Date I

GUIDING
JEWISH YOUTH

SAMUEL M. COHEN

YOUNG PEOPLE'S LEAGUE OF THE UNITED SYNAGOGUE OF AMERICA
NEW YORK
1939

PRINTED IN THE UNITED STATES OF AMERICA
BY THE MARSTIN PRESS, INC.
 439

PREFACE

THE Synagogue is less successful in the work with adolescents than with any other age group in the congregational family. There are proportionately fewer participants enrolled in adolescent activities than in the school, Young People's League, Men's Club, or Sisterhood. Postgraduate classes, Alumni and Bar Mitzvah clubs suffer usually from an alarming mortality, and their members are seldom graduated into the older organizations.

Two principal causes account for the situation. First of all, there is a scarcity of adequate leaders for adolescent groups. While the boys and girls do want to free themselves from adult domination, they cannot get along without adult guidance and stimulation. Unfortunately, it is exceedingly difficult to get the right men and women to give their time and energy to this work, and what is harder still, to undergo the training needed for this delicate and, in a sense, highly technical activity.

The second difficulty is more fundamental. There is very little clear thinking on the aim and purpose of it all. Why adolescent organizations? What specifically are they expected to accomplish with the boys and girls who may constitute their membership? Are proposed objectives psychologically possible? Is the

V

program suggested and carried out in whole or in part
scientifically calculated to advance the organization
towards the realization of its ideals? The lack of
clarity in answering these and similar questions is
responsible for much of the floundering and ineffective-
ness of the efforts in this area.

This book starts with the proposition that the aim of
the Young People's League, the next group in age to
that of adolescence, is the education of its members for
responsibility and leadership in Jewish and civic life.
Education for responsibility must come through the
assumption of responsibility. As a synagogal organization then, the League will desire to share in the conducting of the synagogal institutions. Where shall it
start? What activity can it undertake through which
it may reasonably be expected to contribute an important element in Synagogue life? It is proposed that in
addition to anything else it may do, it should undertake
the organization and the guidance of the adolescents
associated with the Synagogue.

The social stimulation generated by the acceptance
of this project by the League as a whole for this work,
the approval of their colleagues expressed in connection with reports rendered on their progress as well as
the appreciation of adult leaders of the Synagogue will
provide incentives for continued effort. These leaders
will require a theoretical as well as a practical understanding of their task. They will need to know the
nature of the adolescent, his needs, the objectives of
the proposed organization in its synagogal frame of
reference, the techniques of program building and of
treating the manifold problems with which this activity
bristles.

This book is intended to provide a foundation for the study of this phase of the work.

The first four chapters present accepted findings from the psychological and sociological standpoints helpful in discerning those elements in the nature of the adolescent which should affect the aim and program of the adolescent organization.

The next three chapters discuss synagogue life, including the function of worship, and how these may contribute to the development of the program for adolescents. Four chapters follow in which the actual technique of program construction is discussed. Additional chapters on the Program of Sex, the Youth Leader, the Junior Synagogue and the World about it, Constitution, provide additional information and techniques for club leadership.

Two chapters conclude the work. The first is on the Junior Synagogue in action. This consists of a stenographic record of imaginary meetings of various organizations of the Junior Synagogue, exemplifying how some of the more important principles enunciated in the book may actually be expected to operate. The final chapter on Tools is intended to provide a guide for the theoretical and technical literature on the subject that would be of value to leaders of synagogal clubs.

I want to acknowledge my great indebtedness to Professors Adelaide Case and F. Ernest Johnson of Teachers College, Columbia University, for their helpful criticism, constructive suggestions, and stimulating encouragement. I am also grateful to Dr. Julius H. Greenstone, principal of Graetz College of Philadelphia, Pa., and Rabbi Eugene Kohn of New York City for their advice and suggestions. I have also received valuable

advice and help from Mrs. Lillian Sosnow of Hillsdale,
N. J., Miss Annie Fisher of Hartford, Conn., Mrs. Simon
J. Weiner of New York City, Mr. Asher Block and Miss
Helen Rosen.

I am greatly indebted to Dr. Paul Romanoff for his
painstaking reading of the proofs and his many helpful
suggestions.

Finally, I must acknowledge my indebtedness to Mr.
Samuel Frank of Detroit, Mich., without whose interest
and generosity this work would not have been possible.

SAMUEL M. COHEN

New York,
February, 1939

CONTENTS

CHAPTER I

THE NATURE OF ADOLESCENCE

There are now hundreds of thousands of young people leading organized groups of adolescents.* In the Boy Scouts, Girl Scouts, Camp Fire Girls, Young Judaea, and over fifty other national adolescent organizations and movements, millions of boys and girls are guided, directed, coached and helped by young men and women. While older and more mature men and women often make good club leaders, it would seem that for the most part it is the young people who are most successful in working with their still younger brethren.

Perhaps it is due to the fact that the boy or girl feels a greater sense of kinship with young people. The young man is not so far away from him in spirit. They can play together and get the same kind of pleasure out of the game. It may be because the young man or woman enjoys taking youthful charges under his wing, and guiding and directing their development. There is also the inherent idealism of youth that is satisfied apparently to develop and train the character of the boy or girl; to be helpful in educating for virile, spiritu-

*In this book, the terms "adolescents", "youth", and "boys and girls" are used to designate girls from the ages of twelve to seventeen approximately, and boys from the ages of thirteen to eighteen. The term "young people" is used to designate young men and women from the ages of eighteen to twenty-five or thirty.

1

ally-minded citizenship has a strong appeal to many
young people.

In all probability all the above elements play a part
when a young man or woman decides to enter this field.
Club work brings definite satisfactions to those who are
minded to engage in it. Of these, none is stronger than
the enjoyment of the reverential friendship of the club
member who worships his leader as a hero, and whose
love and friendship grows stronger and more valued as
the proportional disparity in the ages of the two
decreases.

The deeper and more enduring satisfactions are
naturally those that come as a result of the more important and vital help rendered the adolescent. If the
object in working with a boy or girl is to give him a
good time, to keep him off the streets, or to prevent
his becoming a delinquent, the benefit accruing will not
be so great, and the happiness of the leader will not be
so deep as when the object is to help develop an individual who will prove to be a useful and valuable member
of society.

The moment the aims of club leadership are conceived
in terms of citizenship, character, and personality, it
becomes evident that the club leader must understand
the nature of the adolescent, especally those dynamic
aspects of his being, that make for a progressive, ethical,
and spiritual life. He needs also to learn something
about the social units in which his charges are to be
integrated, and the ideals and loyalties they are expected increasingly to share.

From this standpoint, the Jewish adolescent presents
both a problem and an opportunity. The Jewish people
are subject everywhere to discrimination and persecu-

tion. The Jewish youth is naturally aware of his disabilities as a Jew, and his developing personality is accordingly subject to destructive influence. On the other hand, he can come into possession of a rich, cultural life shot through with religious and spiritual meaning. If he is made to feel himself part of that life, he may find in the prejudices and disabilities he encounters a challenge that will refine and spiritualize his character.

To lead a Jewish club requires, then, a knowledge of the Jewish adolescent, his nature and problems, and the phases of Jewish life and institutions in which he may be integrated. It also requires knowledge of the culture and institutions that embody the American aspiration for the good life.

This volume is intended to guide the club leader towards obtaining the necessary knowledge and understanding. It will take up those aspects of the nature of adolescents which are significant for one who would work with boys and girls. Their felt needs will be studied from the standpoint of their possible satisfaction in such a way as to make for the awakening of a sense of higher needs and aspirations. It is with respect to these wants that the Jewish religion and institutions will be treated. In general, the student will be encouraged to study Jewish club work as it exists, so that he may learn to discern the principles operating in the methods and programs used in the clubs now in existence, and to apply to them a constructive, critical attitude. He will also be given some guidance in the more technical fields of program construction, and in avoiding or dealing with the more common problems the club leader usually encounters.

The period of adolescence, embracing roughly the
ages of twelve to eighteen is perplexing and difficult both
to the adolescent himself, and to the people about him.
He is subject to sudden and often violent states of feeling. Attraction and repulsion towards persons of the
opposite sex follow each other at unequal and sudden
periods. He is torn between an attiutde of hero worship
towards his parents, and a passion for independence and
self-assertion. Uneven development of the parts of his
body results in many cases in an awkwardness that ac-
centuates his self-conscious and defiant shyness. This
is further aggravated by the unreasonable crushes that
appear at this time.

Various theories have been offered in explanation of
these characteristics. Many believe that the characteristic behavior of adolescents is due entirely to the inner development of the individual. It is his sudden and
rapid growth, physical, emotional and mental, that
is responsible for the strains and stresses that torture
his existence. Investigations and scientific observations
of the mental and emotional traits of the adolescent in
other, simpler cultures than our own show that it is
possible for individuals to pass through this period
without the emotional disturbances that trouble us and
our boys and girls in our civilization. This would
indicate that the difficulties must be equally the result
of our social environment and its demands upon the
developing youth, and of what is taking place within his
own person.

Modern study of the growth of the adolescent supplies a clue to the solution of the riddle. The following
are some authenticated facts, which taken together, are
significant for our purpose.

The height of the child during the adolescent period increases by about 12%. The bony structure of the head grows from 2 to 3%—the brain practically not at all.

Sensitiveness to small differences in color and other sensations is only slightly increased. The elements of intelligence measured by present-day mental tests develop at a less rapid rate than during childhood, until the age of eighteen, when in almost all cases they attain their maximum. Attention, memory, speed of learning and reading increase at about the same date during childhood.

The weight and muscular strength increase at a more rapid pace than before. There occurs a sudden development of the sexual organs, and a stimulation of glandular activity, accompanied by a deepening of the affective and emotional states of the boy and girl.

The above facts take on meaning when it is observed that in some respects the adolescent has almost attained adult stature, and in other respects there is an acceleration of growth toward adulthood. In other words, adolescence marks the stage when the child, as it were, is hurrying towards the attainment of adulthood.

Interest in adults, pleasure in imitating their activities or participating with them is present even in early childhood. When the individual is still some distance from childhood, the interest is naturally not very marked. In adolescence it is as though the boy and girl finds himself within striking distance of the adult world. Just one more spurt, a lengthening of the body, a deepening of the voice, and an attaining of several additional skills—and he is a grown man or woman.

There is accordingly an increased desire for participation in adult life, to make one's contribution as an individual. There is an urge for liberation, independence from adult dominance, not for the purpose of getting out of the adult world, but rather for acquiring the privilege of rendering help, giving cooperation, as an equal. It is in this direction that the boy and girl strives. Unfortunately our present civilization is not adequately prepared to receive the neophyte. Primitive people who sensed what was transpiring in their growing children, developed initiations that actually prepared a child for adulthood. In our more complex culture, the initiation—Bar Mitzvah, or Confirmation—has been dried out and become a mere form. Its connotations are remote from those of the original rites from which it developed. No real effort is made to reckon with the urges and ideals of the boy and girl. Parents insist on maintaining a relationship with their children that was natural only when their offspring were in a state of physical and mental immaturity. They do not yield control without a violent struggle on the part of their boy, and sometimes not even then, stunting the growth of his personality. The main purpose of society in youth guidance has been to provide some training for participation in adult life at a distant future. The present strivings and yearnings of the boy and girl are not regarded as valuable. When the lack of intelligent help on the part of the adult results in a sense of insecurity and consequent anti-social attitudes and deeds, society tries to provide recreational activities to prevent delinquency.

In more recent times there are emerging movements for educating the adolescent by actually creating means through which his interests and capacities may contribute to adult life. It is in this direction that our work should strive. In the case of the Jewish adolescent, our aim should be to develop a form of organization and a program through which he may be increasingly integrated in adult Jewish life as his powers grow and develop. This is another way of stating the objective of this course. The starting point is always the boy and girl. The point of reference is adult Jewish and American life and institutions. The path which we are to prepare for him by means of which the adolescent's approach to the adult is to be made simple and natural, is the club, and the Junior Synagogue.

TOPICS FOR DISCUSSION

1. What characteristic acts or deeds of adolescents indicate a desire for independence from domination of parents or other adults?

2. What acts or deeds indicate a desire to cooperate and help adults?

3. What elements in the program of an A.Z.A. Chapter or a Young Judaea Club are purely recreational, what are a preparation for future adult life, and what represent sharing in adult objectives, and cooperating in their attainment?

REFERENCES

Averill, L. A. *Adolescence*. Pages 48-56, 64-65.

Brooks, Fowler D. *The Psychology of Adolescence*. Pages 18-26, 32-34, 41-44, 62-63, 67-81, 91-105, 109-117.

Hollingworth, Leta S. *The Psychology of the Adolescent*. Pages 19-35.

CHAPTER II

CAPACITIES AND TALENTS

What makes a club meeting interesting? For one thing, the congeniality of the members. When the boys and girls like each other, and enjoy each other's society, the time spent at a club will probably be interesting. The personality of the leader will also play a part. If the members admire and like him, they will look forward to the meeting when they can spend some time together.

Yet it is possible for perfectly good friends to find hours monotonous and boresome. There is a question, too, as to whether the club members do the things the leader advises, because they like him or because some of the activities he fosters answer their needs. It is possible that in the case of the members themselves, the congeniality to each other is due to the fact that there is mutuality of interest in certain activities. When the interest of any of the group turns to a direction different from that of his friends, the ties between him and his friends become affected. He will drift farther and farther away as the time goes on. In other words, the congeniality and leadership may be a result of common interest rather than a cause of it.

Primarily, it is the club activity that must absorb the attention of the boys and girls. What elements usually

9

make up the club program, and under what circumstances will they interest the members? Club meetings
usually consist of several of such activities as the following: Business, arts and crafts, discussions, debates,
recitations, dialogues, musical selections, vocal and instrumental, games, essays, orations, club paper, dances,
dramatics, and refreshments. It is evident that such
activities as refreshments, games and dancing can as a
rule be relied upon. If the appetite is not sated, a snack
or some sweets will have universal appeal. When fatigue
is not present, the challenge of the game will be readily
answered. When the person of the opposite sex is not
repellent for any reason, dancing will prove a delight.
What about such activities as essays, dramatics and
business?

Observers of clubs will find that there is considerable
variety in the amount of interest manifested in the
different elements of the club program. Some activities
absorbing in one club may prove to be deadly in others.
Certain members succeed in rousing the attention of
their club mates better than others. The time and the
occasion of the activity may also play a part. The reading of a selection from "Lamentations" in the course
of a Tishea B'ab program will be attended to better
than at any other time or occasion. The purpose of the
activity is an important factor. When the club journal
is read as an entry in a club paper contest it will evoke
undivided attention.

One factor that must be present if the activity is to
prove interesting, is an ability to engage in it. A girl
assigned to an essay, with no talent for writing, will
not enjoy reaping the fruit of her toil. The audience
will prove even more lethargic. Let a boy with dramatic

talent take a part in a play, and his interest grows. It may even carry over to other club activities. The members of the club will find that part of the program particularly delightful. The abilities or talents of the members are vital factors, though not the only ones in the success of the club program. It is accordingly important to understand something of their nature and functions.

Obviously an aptitude is not a simple ability. We are endowed literally with millions of simple abilities. Every muscle responding to our will, constitutes an ability. Every sensitivity to tone or color, is an ability. In the same category belongs the sensing of relationships, abstract, special or social, known as intelligence. As the infant grows to adulthood, its abilities increase. Maturation in a sense is the development of the full complement of one's abilities in the realms of action, thought, and affection.

Capacities and talents as we perceive them, however, are constituted of complexes, or patterns of the more simple abilities. For instance, the singer must possess a physical endowment; he must have vocal cords of certain length and a certain chest capacity, etc. He needs, in addition, what may be described as mental capacity, ability to discriminate pitch and tone. He requires, also, emotional sensitiveness. Each of these various abilities may exist by itself. When they meet in the one person, they make it possible for him to function as a singer. Consider the stenographer. He must possess certain physical abilities, muscular development of fingers and wrist. He also requires mental abilities in the fields of perception, etc. Intelligence enters here also. These aptitudes may exist independently or they may be combined with other aptitudes in some other pattern. When they exist together, they constitute the stenographer's capacity.

What forces bring about the combining of the various aptitudes in a definite pattern? First of all, there is the social environment which demands certain types of activities on the part of the individual. There is, for instance, a social demand for the ability to play tennis. The individual will accordingly exercise those mental and physical abilities that can combine to constitute a tennis playing pattern. In other words, the pattern is formed with regard to environmental needs. Once formed, it functions as a unit, a talent. There are some combinations that seem to be innate. Musical ability, for instance, appears to run in families. Here, too, however, if there were no social demand for a music pattern, the group of abilities that make it up would either remain unexplored or would form combinations with other abilities, so as to enable the individual to function in other ways.

Under all circumstances there is a primary need for self-expression. Our muscular and mental and emotional abilities must secure an opportunity for exercise. A program of club activities that enables us to give expression to our capacities will interest us, will enrich our lives. Programs that do not call for the exercise of our capacity will be boring, tiring. It is important, then, that our capacities first of all function, and that their exercise result in something that is valued by society. They must provide us with something that we need, to live by, or to receive the approval of our friends and acquaintances.

In developing club programs, then, it is very important that some knowledge be gathered of the abilities and capacity of the children. Without that knowledge, any suggestions as to program would be guessing in the dark.

In the adolescent period, the abilities are not as yet fully developed, and the patterns of talents or aptitudes are as yet vague and changeable. Helpful clues may be obtained from the grades the adolescents get in their school or high school subjects, the private instruction they may be receiving in such subjects as elocution, dramatics or dancing and, what is perhaps more important, the opinion of their playmates. Withal, an open mind must be retained for possible mistakes in estimating the abilities of any particular boy, and for the contingency of a shift of interest and the emerging of a different talent or capacity. A good procedure in beginning to develop a club program is the following:

1. Suggest to the club president the appointment of a program committee, consisting of members who are more intimate with a larger number of their fellow members.

2. Suggest that the committee discuss the interests and aptitudes of the members so that they can form a general idea of the extent to which various abilities are present among the members of the group.

3. Ask the committees to draw up a list of activities possible for club meetings, observances, festivals and club celebrations. Any kind of activity the boys or girls can think of, which may enter into the programs for club gatherings, should be included.

4. Classify the activities by the frequency in which they should be indulged, and the specific aptitudes they would call for, if any.

5. Let the committee compare the talents the activities require, with the list of capacities of the members. Strike out all activities for which there is a lack of boys or girls with appropriate aptitudes.

6. Let the committee decide that the program should conform to the following conditions:

a. Those activities having a general appeal are frequently indulged in.

b. There is variety from meeting to meeting in the activities called for.

c. Every member has an opportunity to participate, or to lead in club work through the exercise of his ability, or abilities.

This procedure will make more certain that every child will have an opportunity to participate in the club program through the utilization of his capacities. The leader should be ready at all times to provide help and encouragement to each child scheduled on the program. Two purposes will be served by this. It will insure a well prepared program. Even when the child has talents in a given direction, he may still need encouragement and guidance so that his efforts will be most fruitful.

In the second place, it will give the leader the opportunity to note promptly any change of interest taking place, and enable him to suggest changes in assignments and contents of programs.

TOPICS FOR DISCUSSION

1. What simpler elements are components of the following capacities: acting, esthetic dancing, literary criticism, coaching a football team?

2. What are the rewards and satisfactions, personal and social, following success in the exercise of the above capacities?

3. Diagnose the following situations, suggesting remedial procedures:

a. The club is challenged to a debate. After some effort, a team is organized. The members are slow in their preparatory readings. Attendance at team conferences is irregular. The debate is lost, and the members of the team drop out of the club.

b. The parents of the members are, on the whole, uneducated working people. Their principal interests seem to be card-playing, movies, parties, and an occasional theatrical performance. The members of the club are interested only in dancing and parties, at which there are parlor games, deriving their interest from the mutual attraction of the sexes. The business meetings are not taken seriously—there are whispering, giggling, and occasional flares of quarreling—yet the children are doing well in high school.

REFERENCES

Averill, L. A. *Adolescence*. Pages 185-187, 203-214.

Brooks, Fowler D. *The Psychology of Adolescence*. Pages 275-306.

Jersild, Arthur T. *Child Psychology*. Pages 287-291, 327-329, 398-407.

CHAPTER III

ASPIRING TO ADULTHOOD

Club life answers to a number of felt wants of the child. It provides him with a group of friends with whom he could cooperate in pleasure-giving undertakings. The ties of friendship encourage reciprocal confidences, sharing of interests, information, plans, and aspirations. There is competition, rivalry, emulation and triumph, personal and group—the emotional concomitants of vitality, of life. The activities yielding these results also make for growth and development—physical, mental and emotional.

There are also activities that answer to another equally important need, that appear to have a purpose outside of the boy or girl, outside the club. Some clubs organize dances for which a small price of admission is charged. The proceeds go either to meet some of the club expenses in connection with its work, or the entertainment of its members. There are times when the profits are used, in whole or in part, as a contribution for some charitable or welfare cause. Some clubs make special collections for welfare or educational purposes. Others allot a part of the dues received. Many a club will make regular monthly contributions for the synagogue or center housing them.

Very frequently, a number of adolescent groups cooperate by means of a club council. Each club appoints or elects representatives that form a council. The powers of this super-organization varies from community to community, and its activities run accordingly from preventing conflict, to arranging for cooperative enterprises, to controlling the life and the program of the individual club. In this area, too, the individual's interests tend to emerge from himself and his group into wider spheres, larger groupings.

The sense of connectedness with the outside world is expressed in one or more of the following activities:

Arrangements for entertainments for other clubs, for parents of the members, or more generally, for the adult members of the congregation; participation in flag, flower or tag days; participation in adult religious services by contribution to its content; participation in civic community enterprises.

There are also activities which indicate an interest in the same cultural or social institutions developed in the adult world. The business of the club is conducted in accordance with the forms and standards set by adults. The members will often arrange festival celebrations by themselves and for themselves. They will conduct worship exercises for themselves. Some clubs encourage creative activities in agriculture, and arts and crafts, for pecuniary purposes. There is many a group bound together by a common interest in scientific experimentation.

Some of the club activities derive their interest principally from the fact that they enable the children to behave like adults irrespective of the objectives of the acts. It is doubtful whether the younger children realize the values of parliamentary procedure. Making motions, calling points of order, consulting the Constitution, etc., are things adults are doing all the time in their organizations. It is pleasant to do the same, even though at times these things may interfere with vital club work. similarly, much of the pleasure of conducting their own services is derived from the feeling that they are behaving like adults, though there is also present some pleasure in engaging in the pageantry of the exercises—the joining in the singing, and in the expression of a dimly felt need for communion with the divine.

This however never constitutes the sole purpose of the activity. In addition to the make-believe, there is the actual expression of growing powers which can be exercised through the pattern of action. That itself is pleasurable, even though the larger purposes for which they may be used are still beyond recognition.

Other activities are expressions of adult wants. Scientific experimentation brings the joys of discovery and achievement. Business enterprise, agricultural undertakings, etc. are cast in miniature adult form, and their driving power is the same that motivates grown-ups. Still other activities express a desire to help adults. The rewards are approval and the feeling of security in knowing that there is authority approving of one's deeds. There are still other undertakings made expressly for the purpose of cooperating with adults. The actual purpose of the undertakings is partly or wholly shared by the boys and girls, and they enjoy the feeling that they are working side by side with their parents for objectives regarded by both child and grown-up as worthwhile.

These, then, are the ways in which aspiration toward adult life finds expression in club activities. The members try to act like adults, to satisfy maturing adult urges, to obtain approval of authorities on whom they depend for some activity, to help adults, and finally to cooperate with adults. Some activities find their value in only one of the above ways. Others are effective from several directions. Generally speaking, acting like adults and satisfying the dawning adult interests are valuable for self-development. Cooperation with adults and with each other makes for the development of the personality in the social sense. Helping adults or seeking adult approval is less valuable than cooperative activities.

The last chapter has considered one principle that may be applied in evaluating club programs—the capacities for the natural equipment of the individual should be utilized to the utmost. There has been some criticism of club programs from this standpoint. Suggestions have been made for procedures by which the aptitudes of the adolescents can be effectively utilized. From the discussion in this chapter, we derive another equally important standard. How effectively does a program train for participation in adult life? What opportunities does it offer for such participation? Is the club an entering wedge in adult life, or is it kept distinct as a play world in which the members make believe they are adults—modern, ancient, or primitive.

There is another principle which deserves a word at this time. There are two ways of conceiving present-day adult institutions or movements towards which the boy is expected to develop loyalties. They may be regarded as set, fixed, or static. When they are so regarded, the sole purpose of the club is to do its share in molding the boy and girl into a cog of the adult wheel of action. On the other hand, these institutions may be considered as being themselves subject to progressive change, or retrogressive decay. If so, it would devolve upon the club also to lay foundations for developing a constructive, critical attitude to these organizations, institutions and movements. What norms should the child develop for evaluating present day adult culture?

For the present, let us note the principal institutions through which adults function. To facilitate consideration, they may be divided into the following categories: vocational, civic, social, religious. In Jewish life the institutions serving one or more of the above principal needs, take on a different character from those serving similar needs of the general community. This is due to the past experience of the Jew and his rich heritage, as well as to his present anomalous status.

Vocational institutions or activities are those which exist for the purpose of contributing to the wealth, welfare, pleasure or security of fellow human beings, with the object of obtaining returns in goods and finance, to be used for the same purposes by the individual concerned. What with the prejudices and discriminations now extant in practically every part of the world, the vocational problems of the Jew are intensified and multiplied.

Civic institutions and activities exist for the mutual well-being and protection of the civic community, whether it be rural or urban, state or county. Now, in addition to the duty of the Jew to his country, and the need for his full-hearted participation in its life, the Jew is possessed of a culture and spiritual heritage of unique value which he must preserve. The misunderstandings and enmities he encounters create a need for institutions making for education and cooperation with non-Jewish organizations, for the purpose of creating mutual understanding and appreciation. Actual injury, economic and physical, inflicted on Jews in different parts of the world necessitate worldwide movements and organizations dedicated to relief, welfare and reconstruction.

Social institutions or activities function in expressing, creating and deepening friendships. Such institutions are in a sense civic in nature, though they lack external force behind them. Here, too, the Jew has his own problems in addition to those he shares with the non-Jew.

Religious institutions are concerned with providing a dynamic philosophy of life, and integrating human effort from the standpoint of an all-embracing ideal and insipration. The major religions find such integrative principles in the concept of the brotherhood of Man and the fatherhood of God. The Jew has naturally developed out of his nature and experience a wealth of literature, doctrine, custom, law and ceremony through which he can best express his religious aspirations.

This classification, it must be emphasized, is not a reflection of life in reality. Many activities or institutions function to a greater or lesser degree in one or more of the ways enumerated. The classification is used only for the purpose of facilitating our thinking in those fields.

The basic needs of humanity may be constant, but the institutions by which those needs are satisfied change as civilization changes and develops. For a long time it was thought that a child lives through past forms of civilization and that the best preparation for modern living is his being kept immersed in former stages of culture during childhood. Many adolescent organizations accordingly incorporate some primitive form of life as the pattern to which the children are made to conform. A number of clubs ask the children to live in a primitive Indian or explorer pattern. They learn many skills and attain achievements formerly useful, but now much less essential. Many Jewish adolescents organize themselves on a tribal basis and conform with what is supposed to be the primitive Jewish tribal organization.

Is this necessary? Is the theory on which this form of organization is founded true to accepted scientific fact?

On the other hand, it would not be true to say that the cultural patterns of the past have no value for the present life of the boy or girl. Primitive life calls for less developed intellectual power, and presents simpler problems than modern life. It accordingly makes an adequate culture for the play life of the adolescent. There may also be some value in the vivid way in which such dramatizations enable the boy to re-live past heroic experiences and accomplishments of the race. Some national organizations and programs endeavor to use dramatizations for this purpose.

Ultimately, though, the club must provide approaches for actually entering adult life, and adult Jewish life. What specifically shall the club program contain to effect this end?

In the vocational field the following activities are helpful: Members may engage in a number of fundraising activities for various social, educational and philanthropic purposes. The work undertaken should be within the realm of their understanding and interest. Earning money by rendering real service, making useful articles and selling them, preparing an entertainment justifying admission charges, and similar enterprises provide training in business procedure and methods which are of use in adult life. Agricultural projects, arts and crafts, dramatics, literary and musical activities, provide opportunities for exploring one's interests and aptitudes. Sincerely conducted, they have great vocational value. Many organizations provide an extensive system of honors and rewards to encourage wide-spread exploration by these media. It is doubtful whether equally good results cannot be obtained without these rewards. Activities integrated in a general program may be more valuable.

Essays, readings and lectures by representatives of various professions on the satisfactions and difficulties inherent in their respective occupations are also helpful. Care must be taken, though, that the emphasis be on the actual work involved in the occupation, rather than on the extrinsic rewards that may come to those who engage in it.

In the civic areas, American and Jewish, a host of activities suggest themselves. There may be celebrations of national holidays, such as Independence Day, Decoration Day, Armistice Day, Thanksgiving Day, Lincoln and Washington Birthdays. Through these celebrations there may be brought out effectively the value of some of the more cherished American institutions. Addresses from officers and officials representing various civic departments, excursions to points of historic and civic interests are also helpful. In addition, the boys and girls can participate in some of the civic

functions, such as management of the children's traffic
on school and club days, participation in Safety Week,
Fire Prevention Week, etc. From the Jewish standpoint there can be contributions in the form of money
or services, or both, for the Jewish institutions and
movements.

Many elementary religious schools have instituted
what is known as the Keren Ami project. The pupils
contribute a weekly stipend which adds up to a sizable
sum by the end of the year. Then for a short period the
children are told by word of mouth or through their
school paper of a number of causes or institutions that
require aid. A large meeting is arranged at which the
value and importance of these movements are presented
in the form of addresses by selected pupils. A vote de-
termines the proportions in which the money is to be
divided for the various causes.

This procedure, it is thought, will habituate the
children to sacrifice for worthwhile causes, and will
acquaint them with the nature and value of various
movements and institutions.

A number of criticisms have been leveled with reason
against this project. It has been pointed out that the
children make no real sacrifice in making their contributions since the money they give cannot possibly have
the same meaning for them that it has for adults. In
the second place it is doubtful whether the complex and
sometimes abstract nature of modern movements and
institutions can be grasped by the children whose com-
prehension of social phenomena and obligations is
naturally limited. It was questioned finally whether the
procedure does not encourage a destructively critical
attitude toward some important institutions. Does it

not convey the feeling that the institutions that do not win in the vote may be legitimately neglected?

With some modification, however, the project may have value for adolescents. The discussions with reference to the Jewish movements should not be tied up with the undertakings to aid one movement or another. They should be limited to the institutions in each field: defense, welfare, education, Palestine, etc.—rather than the comparison of the value of the fields themselves. It is advisable, for instance, to discuss the relative merits of the Jewish Congress movement and the American Jewish Committee. It would not be advisable to compare the various merits of a movement in the defense area, such as the American Jewish Committee, with an institution in the educational field, such as Dropsie College.

The social life of the club is fostered by every cooperative activity—games, dancing, mutual hospitality, cooperation with non-Jewish groups—all serving to extend and deepen social ties.

Every group activity that helps to increase and strengthen the social ties of its members tends to satisfy their religious need. Many of the forms and ceremonies through which these relationships are expressed are of a religious nature.

Discussion of the forces within and without, frustrating their social ideals, will help motivate the worship expressing the need of and aspiration to communion with the divine.

Many of the above suggestions do not necessitate changes in the form of the club program. They provide concrete and meaningful content to the forms. Other suggestions require special committees that do their work outside of the club meetings, but are responsible for their results to the club as a whole. Some of the activities proposed are suitable for the individual club —others for a council of clubs, or the Junior Synagogue. In organizing these club programs, these suggestions should be carefully studied and utilized to the greatest possible extent.

TOPICS FOR DISCUSSION

1. By what standards shall club activities be evaluated? Which of these standards are within the understanding of an adolescent?

2. Suppose you wanted to make a survey of the club—what questions would you ask about it that would give you the necessary information, on the basis of which you could give constructive criticism?

3. Consider the program of an existing club you know, or are able to make a study of, and criticize it from the standpoint of the principles outlined in this chapter.

REFERENCES

Averill, L. A. *Adolescence*. Pages 121-122, 409-419.

Cohen, Samuel M. *The Progressive Jewish School*. Pages 37-40.

Hollingworth, Leta S. *The Psychology of the Adolescent*. Pages 59-62, 77-91, 148-150, 157-164.

Wieman, Regina Westcott, *The Modern Family and the Church*. Pages 246-248, 256-257, 265.

CHAPTER IV

THE INTEGRATION AND GROWTH
OF PERSONALITY

It is clear by this time that the principal urge of the adolescent is to enter adult life and that the principal usefulness of the club is to facilitate a progressively larger participation on the part of the members in adult activities and institutions. It is the function of the leader so to guide the boys and girls in their club work as to make the club most helpful from this standpoint.

We have studied several important aspects of adolescent psychology and of adult life and have developed as a result, a number of methods and suggestions to be incorporated in the club program. In due course we will gather these suggestions, study and organize them for the purpose of presenting an adequate program of club work. Before proceeding with this task we must consider other aspects of the nature of adolescence and of adult life that will lead to additional suggestions and a further enrichment of the program we are constructing.

Let us today consider the adult world a little more closely. Should we have said world? Do adults live in one, or more than one, world? Consider there is the home and family. This is a compact little world to which we are attached by strong ties that influence much of our feelings and actions. These ties result also in what we may call norms or standards of conduct with respect to the various members of the family circle. There are demands and sacrifices made in this world that are seldom made outside. Each member of the family seems to have a place which governs to some degree his relationship, feelings and conduct, with respect to the other members.

There is also our circle of friends and here we seem to live really in more than one circle, depending on the source, history and nature of the friendships. In these worlds we develop norms and standards that differ sometimes radically from those existing in the family. We expect more, less, or different things from our friends.

There are other worlds. There is the business world; the professional world; the club, political, social or civic; the labor, business or craft organizations to which we may belong. Fraternal organizations demand loyalty and treatment of the members one to the other that differ in part from the demands of other groups. The neighborhood, the city, the state and the country enmesh us in tenuous but powerful webs which at times may prove strong enough to exact from us our wealth, well-being, and even, our lives. Many of us profess also a loyalty to humanity as a whole. There are churches and religious bodies. Nor must we forget the institutions and movements through which constructive and corrective measures are advanced, aiming to implement the aspiration for human well-being and happiness.

Instances are philanthropic, social welfare, and educational institutions.

Every world in adult life has its own code of ethics, its own standard of conduct. Some of these standards explicitly apply also to our other relationships. Since there are wide and varied differences among these codes, there must be conflict.

The business code permits advertising. Certain professional codes do not. Defense of people we know to be guilty is frowned upon in ordinary life. A lawyer is in duty bound, when assigned to a case, to use every means within the law to protect the man he may know to be a criminal. In the everyday world, accumulation of money often results in attainment of high social position. Religious and ethical norms make for a careful examination of the methods used in accumulating wealth, and the use made of it. At the present time there is a tendency to evaluate also the results of large accumulations of wealth in themselves.

Even in adolescence the individual suffers from these conflicts. The code set up for him in the family differs from the practices he finds on the street among his friends. His parents often expect him to abide by standards of behavior which they transgress openly or in secret. His religious school advocates certain standards; in the street, others prevail. His friends expect certain loyalties, sacrifices, and efforts on their behalf, which sometimes are in conflict with what is taught in religious school, and what is expected by the family. As a result of these conditions there is much inner conflict, unhappiness, and danger of neurosis or delinquency.

One way of solving the problem may be the involve-

ment of the indivdual in one particular loyalty to the
exclusion of any other. We can see instances of tendencies in this direction both in the past and in the present. The strong loyalties to family, existing in certain
regions in America, which have resulted in the past in
deadly feuds, may be taken as examples of cases where
the family has become the exclusive world of the individual. Everything else about him is valued only to
the extent to which it contributes to family welfare
and prestige. The efforts of the Fascists to make the
State dominate every phase of the life of its subjects,
is another instance of one world being regarded as
possessing exclusive rights over every interest or loyalty.

This method of attacking the problem must fail for
a very simple reason. There is a real psychological and
practical basis for the other loyalties. It is true that
we possess a natural love for our families but it is
equally natural to love friends, people and humanity.
If attempts are made to suppress the latter attach-
ments, difficulties must ensue.

There is need of the recognition of the naturalness
and rightness of a variety of loyalties, through the
establishing of an adequate relationship between them.
In other words, if a hierarchy of loyalties were established, with some loyalties occupying a definite position in the life of the individual, having specific reference to other loyalties, integration may be secured. But
which loyalty shall head this hierarchy? Shall the family, state, business organizations, or humanity be
placed in supreme command? A little reflection will
show that it is only love of humanity that can occupy
this position. Love of humanity includes love of family,

love of fellow citizens. It limits the expression of the
loyalties to the lesser groups to such forms as would
not be contrary to the love of humanity, but such
limitations cannot be regarded as diminishing the loyalties to the smaller groups. On the contrary, these
limitations are in reality an enrichment of these loyalties. It gives point, aim, and direction to these loves.
Why be faithful to our families? Because our family
can be of service to the state, to humanity. Its achievements in the service of humanity are a justification for
the maintenance and the defense of the state. What is
America's great pride? Its upholding of the ideals of
democracy and its development of invention and in-
dustry from which the world as a whole benefits.

The integration of personality demands the incul-
cation of loyalty to the cause of humanity as a whole,
in which other loyalties may have their place.

Here a word of warning is necessary. There is a
tendency nowadays to invent fine slogans to which
many of us give lip service, with little or no effect upon
our conduct. Love of humanity is such a slogan. We
like to proclaim, exhort and expound it, but are little
affected by what happens to the indivdual men, women
and children that make up humanity. Some men will
say that they are internationalists, loving far and distant peoples, and evidencing no concern for the well-
being of those who are near and dear to them. This is
not internationalism. Love of humanity is more than
love of family, but it must not take the place of more
intense loyalties. On the contrary, it must take on the
characteristics of the more limited loyalties. In a word,
loyalty to humanity must be more than a pure verbal-
ism. Charity must be more than an act responding to

an abstract sense of duty. Human warmth and understanding should permeate altruistic deeds.

It is also necessary to realize that in forming the
higher loyalties there is no surrender of the narrower
affections and interests. Concepts like state and nation,
and humanity must not be set up as gods that enslave
their subjects. The justification for loyalty to the
state is that through it the vital needs of the indivdual
can best be met. It is well similarly to foster the establishing of organizational machinery through which
groups, states and nations may cooperate solely to
advance the well-being of the constituent groups.

The loyalties to the organizational machine need not
supersede the loyalties to the smaller groups or to himself. These aspects of his self are not in contradiction.
His personality grows as his social vision and social integration develop. The value of his social activities is
derived from the resulting enrichment of his personality.

What can the club do to deepen or develop the
higher loyalties? What means are available to it? How
shall these means be used?

Integration of personality may be conceived from another, a more elemental viewpoint. A newly born infant
gives the impression of a fairly unintegrated being.
His movements are random, and for the most part uncoordinated. Pinching one part of the body will result
in a general restlessness of the whole organism, with
no effort to protect the affected part. Even the eyes
are uncoordinated, left and right eye moving in different directions at the same time. Integration begins
when the objective, aim or purpose of the action begins to control. In every instance it is as though some

objective acts as superior to other possible aims, with the result that movements are organized, coordinated to serve its purpose.

The type of objective that has this power is usually one that serves the end of a more vital part of the organism, or of the organism as a whole. Every organ, every muscle, every nerve, while connected and related to every other part of the organism, is possessed with an energy of its own, and the consequent need of self-expression. Sweets are pleasant, and the taking of food is satisfying. Muscularization gives pleasure, and even the sensations of anger and fear may be sought after. Yet conscious restraint is necessary if indulgence in appetite is not to lead to injury to the organism as a whole, and if the action of the individual is not to prevent the interaction with a social environment necessary also for the security and happiness of the individual. From the very start, social and physical restraint in some direction and encouragement in others, is exercised by the men and women about the child. This enables it to direct and control its acts, appetites and feelings so that they may answer to his deeper and more vital physical and social needs.

It must be noted, though, that the integration of the indivdual is not due solely to the external factors operating. The more inclusive objectvies which can control the expression of appetite can also determine its strength. Too much indulgence in sweets will affect the sensitivity of the taste nerve ends. The body as a whole will react when the exercise of a part threatens its well-being, but the reaction may be imperfect or too late. Help from parents and friends is very useful. Similarly, the organism possesses the equipment with which it may interact with its social environment and it can and does associate its own welfare with the welfare of a social group. But here, its need for help from without is even more pronounced.

The individual is happiest when he can identify social needs with his own. This achievement requires naturally an expanding and deepening sense of relationship with a social environment. As his powers mature, the interaction comes more easily and can be made more meaningful. As the objectives of the relationships with the environment rise to higher planes and extend to wider areas, the personality develops and grows.

Various institutions have evolved through which the socialization of the child is fostered and the higher ideals of life are implemented. The home and family, the church and religious school, the state and its secular educational system, all aim in this direction, differing from each other largely in the age levels at which they serve, and the segments of life that constitute their concern. These differences, though, are indistinct, and duplication and conflict often ensues.

Religion has been manifest in every part of the world, and in historic time it has always fostered the highest and most embracing human ideals. While religious organizations have often proven narrow and faltering, the religious impulse has been vital and made its impress upon the life of the individual and the family. Even the state and other non-religious institutions have had to accept some of its principles. When organizations created to advance religious objectives become narrow and subservient to selfish ends and institutions, the religious impulse has from time to time modified the organizations or destroyed them and re-created them in new form.

The club should align itself definitely with the religious forces in life through affiliation with a religious institution. While it is true that a tendency of the synagogue in the recent past has been to narrow its function to the rituals and ceremonies of worship, there is evidence now of the return to its former position as a source of religious influence on life as a whole. The congregational school aims more and more to prepare the child for entrance into the adolescent organization. The Young People's League is the association towards which every boy and girl will aspire—because it aims more directly to educate its members for responsibility and leadership in Jewish life, institutions and movements. When the members of the league grow older, they will naturally enter the adult institutions of the congregation which maintains the synagogue.

TOPICS FOR DISCUSSION

1. Why is youth idealistic, and why are youthful ideals destroyed when one grows older?

2. Do social situations control physical appetites or desires? Give instances.

3. Discuss the value of social and athletic clubs.

4. Give instances of good sportsmanship. Discuss their value.

REFERENCES

American Association of School Administrators. Sixteenth Yearbook of the American Association of School Administrators, pages 232-257.

Brooks, Fowler D. *The Psychology of Adolescence.* Pages 416-430, 475-477.

38 GUIDING JEWISH YOUTH

Cohen, Samuel M. *The Progressive Jewish School*. Pages 5-6, 7-10.

Groves, Ernest R. *Personality and Social Adjustment*. Pages 156-175.

Hollingworth, Leta S. *The Psychology of the Adolescent*. Pages 165-177, 183-185.

Young, Paul Thomas. *Motivation of Behavior*. Pages 388-399, 408-416.

Wieman, Regina Westcott. *The Modern Family and the Church*. Pages 249-251.

CHAPTER V

SYNAGOGUE LIFE

Several considerations stand out from the material presented in the last chapter. 1. There is a definite need for the growth and integration of the self and personality. 2. The individual is equipped physically, mentally and emotionally for the socialization of himself, the growth of his personality. Since he undergoes a process of maturation, the extent of his attainments in this direction is limited by the state of his development. Complete fulfillment can be attained only when the individual is matured. 3. Society has developed a number of institutions which express or answer to the needs of the human being for socialization. Unfortunately most of these institutions confine themselves to certain aspects of these needs, and do not foster the more embracing loves and loyalties, with the result that they effect a splitting of the personality, with consequent injuries to the individual and society. 4. It is possible, though, so to conceive the function of many of these institutions as to enable them to contribute to the development of the higher personality. By regarding them as preparatory steps towards the ideal rather than as ends in themselves, much of the conflicts in life may be removed. This may necessitate radical changes

in the constitution and ideology of these institutions.
5. Religion is the name given to the phenomena in life
descriptive of human striving for the development of the
higher integrating ideals, loves and loyalties. In their
ultimate form they represent reverence for and loyalty
to God. In this area, too, institutions have been created
to serve this purpose. Judaism, the religion of the Jew,
has its own standards, codes, forms, dogma, ceremonials, festivals, and ritual of worship. Through them the
Jew expresses his higher aspirations, and obtains the
strength necessary to live the better life. In the diaspora, the central institution through which Judaism functions, is the Synagogue.

In this chapter we will consider more carefully the
ways in which the Synagogue can function to this end,
and how this can further enrich the club program.

The origin of the Synagogue is veiled in the distant
past. Reference to the Synagogue as an important
functioning institution is found in works dated from
the days of the Second Commonwealth. Throughout
the diaspora, until very recently, the Synagogue has
served as the center of Jewish life. It was more than a
place of prayer and worship. All activities of the Jewish community emanated from the Synagogue. It often
housed the school, secondary school, and adult educational activities. The last mentioned, which are quite
new to western civilization, were widespread in Israel.
Even the unlettered Jew was wont to listen in the Synagogue on the Sabbath and weekday afternoons to
translations and homiletical interpretations of parts
of the prayer book, the psalms, other parts of the
Bible, and the agadic portions of the Talmud. The
Synagogue was also the house of assembly. The more

important business of the community was as a rule
decided at the Synagogue. Many charitable and welfare institutions such as the hospital, the home for the
aged, and the orphan asylum originated in the Synagogue and were often housed in it.

All vital events in the life of the individual, such as
Bar Mitzvah, marriage and death found suitable ceremonials in the Synagogue. Synagogue worship, in fact,
embraces a large number of elements variously combined for different purposes.

The following elements may be distinguished in the
traditional Jewish Prayer Book. 1. Many parts are
dramatizations of the worship activities of the ancient
Israelites. There is an effort to strengthen the memory
of the Temple worship by reciting some of the psalms
and prayers uttered during those sacrifices. On the Day
of Atonement some of the Temple ceremonies are re-
produced. The action of the High Priest and the as-
sembled congregation in the Temple courts is re-
enacted by the cantor and congregation in the synagogue. This phase of Jewish worship helps to convey
the sense of the continuity of the past and present
generations. 2. The Services contain also selected
Biblical or talmudic material for study. Study of the
sacred literature was regarded as a form of worship, a
means of drawing closer to the Divine. 3. There are
also homiletic elements, including the sermon, through
which ancient ideas and ideals are applied to modern
problems. 4. The exercises are intended to be helpful
in meeting the felt problems of the day. When a great
calamity befell the Jew, the sorrow and prayer it
evoked found appropriate expression in Liturgical
poetry. Poems evoking deep and vital thoughts and

feelings were often included in the prayers, and retained long after the events referred to had been superseded by other happenings. The exercises contain elements that in a sense reflect the spiritual prayers and aspirations of the Jew, from the ancient past to comparatively recent times. 5. The order of worship embraces also, direct supplications for forgiveness of everyday sins and transgressions, and prayers for everyday needs, health, sustenance, security, and happiness. It is noteworthy that many of these prayers refer to the needs of the Jewish people as a whole, rather than those of the indivdual. In this way the ritual of worship emphasizes the integration of the individual with his people. There is also the injunction that it is more meritorious to worship in the company of nine others than by oneself. A group of ten is regarded as adequate for giving the impression of a community. One worships more adequately as a member of the community than as an individual.

Nothing illustrates so aptly the way in which all Jewish life is echoed and enriched in Synagogue life, as the Sabbath and festival services. The Jewish festivals date back to dim antiquity, retaining the spiritual core of their ancient meaning. They have associated with themselves legends, historic events and new meanings harmonious with the original emotion that gave them birth. In this way every festival is rich with historic association and ethical import. The principal features are the following:

The Sabbath

The Sabbath has occupied a position of supreme importance in the Jewish calendar. The social and religious ceremonies marking its observance bear the imprint of the vital experiences of the Jewish people through the ages. The thoughts and ideals associated with it attain the highest level of Jewish aspiration.

The establishment of the Sabbath is associated with the story of the Creation as told in the Bible with its emphasis on the inherent goodness of the world and the divine element in man. The observance of the Sabbath stresses accordingly the unique value of human personality. In harmony with this ideal it is a memorial to the liberation from Egyptian bondage, a symbol of freedom and liberty. The Sabbath is a day of delight and happiness derived from the sense of fellowship in fostering and expressing the higher human values.

The ritual of the Sabbath services express various aspects of these ideals enriched by Jewish experiences. The *Oneg Shabos*, the delight of the Sabbath, is a name given to the social gatherings on Sabbath afternoon or Friday evening, revived with the restoration of Palestine. Refreshments are served. There may be an address and discussion on some Jewish or ethical subject. There is singing and in the case of boys and girls there may also be games.

Sukkot

Sukkot was originally celebrated at the close of the harvest season, when preparations are made for the insurance of a new harvest the coming year. It is observed by dwelling in tabernacles, the giving of tithes, contributions for the poor, and the maintenance of the religious cult. It is a time also for thanksgiving, for the blessings of the fruit of the soil, which satisfy the fundamental needs of mankind. Some of the pertinent meaning of the events associated with Sukkot are the following:

1. The festival is associated with the liberation from Egypt, inasmuch as the Israelites dwelt in "sukkahs" (booths) on leaving Egypt.

2. In this connection it is well to bear in mind some of the implications of the ceremony. The sukkah is physically weak, flimsy, a dwelling place that induces a feeling far from that of safety or security. The consciousness, however, of being in consonance with God's will assures strength and safety even in the sukkah. The roof of the dwelling must be constructed so that the stars and sky may be visible. Security is not obtained in complete isolation and separation from the world. The consciousness of God in the world gives the world, as a whole, the character of a home.

3. In our thanksgiving we are especially mindful of the foliage of Palestine and make use in our celebration of *esrog, lulav, hadassim* and *aravot*.

4. These plants, the *esrog, lulav, hadassim* and *aravot* differ from each other. Their being united makes the joy possible. The Rabbis dwell on this fact to emphasize the importance of unity among the varied elements that make up the Jewish people; the scholar and the ignoramus, the saint and the sinner, all must be united. Union itself is ennobling.

5. During the festival period, in ancient Judea, there was a special ceremony marking the transition from idolatry to the worship of one God. The *Simhat bet hashoeva* was made significant, according to the Rabbis, by the fact that the prayers for rain and the observances were directed to the West, where the Ark

stood, rather than the East, where the sun was. The rejoicing may be taken to be the result of our confidence in God's love.

6. The period is one during which the various tithes were distributed, the gifts by which the sacerdotal institutions were maintained and poverty and misery relieved. This, too, added to the joy in the land.

Hanukkah

1. Hanukkah commemorates the victories of the outnumbered and ill-equipped Maccabeans against the powerful Syrian army. It can stimulate pride in Jewish ancestry and the will to battle for one's faith and people.

2. Admiration for ability to suffer martyrdom for one's faith is aroused by the story of Hannah and her Seven Sons.

3. The element emphasized in the festival ceremony is the rededication of the Temple and the maintaining of the perpetual light. The Temple is the source of physical as well as spiritual strength. As the prophets have always maintained, material strength, prosperity and safety come only with the righteous life.

4. The legend of the perpetual light points to the fact that even when the difficulties of living the spiritual life seem insurmountable, the effort should be made nevertheless. There is a power that helps the light to shine if we are ready to make our own contribution.

5. Hanukkah comes at a time when the winter solstice is near. The Feast of Lights points to the fact that man can counteract the phenomena naturally

harmful to him. He can under certain limitations rise above nature.

The lights of Hanukkah represent in Jewish theology the spiritual light with which the religious institutions, the Temple and the Synagogue are effulgent. The period is one in which the purification and the rededication of the Temple are commemorated. Hanukkah is, accordingly, suitable for strengthening reverence for the Synagogue. The heroism of the Maccabees is operative today if it expresses itself as a resolution to make sacrifices for the furthering of the Synagogue and its institutions.

Hamisha Asar Beshvat

The day marks the beginning of the new year for the trees of Palestine, when their annual cycle of growth, efflorescence and fruition begins. By making this an occasion for celebration, the Jew shows his affiliation with the Holy Land. In modern times the festival has become meaningful by including the Jewish hope for rehabilitation of Palestine as its national homeland.

Purim

Purim is a festival dedicated essentially to the conception of the unity of Israel and the responsibility that each member bears for the other. Haman's hatred for Mordecai is expressed by his desire to annihilate all the Jews. Esther is exhorted to regard her elevation to the throne as justified solely by the opportunity it gives her to be of service to those who remained in the ranks. She risks her life in visiting Ahasuerus only on condition that all Israel fast and pray for her.

Passover

Passover is one of the most ancient of Jewish festivals. It is almost impossible to exhaust the ideas and ideals, sentiments and feelings that combine to make up its glowing texture. Some of the more important are the following:

1. It celebrates the liberation of Israel and emphasizes the injustice of enslavement and oppression.

2. It is the national birthday of the Jewish people and is an appropriate occasion for expressing the joy of the birthday and for emphasizing the peculiar character of the Jew in choosing the good life.

3. Fundamentally, it is a family festival and is a fit time to emphasize the happiness that comes from expressing filial affection.

4. The Passover festival has ever been associated with faith in God as a protector. The first night of Passover is called night of vigil. Innumerable stories are told of how threatening danger was dispelled at that time by God's watchful care over Israel.

5. It is also associated with numerous false accusations against the Jewish people.

6. It marks the coming of spring, and is a time for the tender, sweet happiness of the season, the call of new plant life.

7. It marks the beginning of the counting of the Omer, directing attention to Shabuot, the fulfillment of the promise to achieve union with the Divine.

8. The life of Moses, his heroism, humility, persistence, devotion and the innumerable legends that have

clustered about him all can be made into sources of inspiration.

Lag-Ba-Omer

The origin of this festival is veiled in the distant past. The legends that cluster about it emphasize the following elements: The joy of the school child when freed from disease or danger, and his happiness in the ability to enjoy the outdoors; the victory over those who would prevent the study of Judaism; the end of the winter season.

Shabuot

The Shabuot festival marks the beginning of the summer. It is the Hag ha-Bikkurim, the festival of the first fruits, and expresses the gratitude and joy of the ripening fields. In ancient days the Israelites brought their first fruits to the Temple in expression of their gratitude to the Divine.

The central theme of the Holy Day is the first covenant between God and Israel consummated at Mount Sinai when the Israelites experienced the revelation of Divine Law. In a sense this was a fulfillment of the promise made to Moses when he received the call to deliver the Jews from the Egyptians, "when thou hast brought forth the people out of Egypt, ye shall serve God upon this mountain". The analogy evidently should be made with the natural phenomenon of the first fruits realizing the promise that was in the sowing of the seed.

The *Book of Ruth* is read in the synagogues on this day. The devotion of Ruth to Judaism and the Jewish people, and the story of the gleanings left for the poor, are in harmony with the feeling-tone of Shabuot.

The club activities expressing and enriching the ideals

and feelings associated with the various festivals permit of infinite variety. Such activities may take the form of intimate celebrations confined to one club. They may consist of programs given for a guest club. They may constitute the contribution of the club to the program of the whole Junior Synagogue. They may constitute a celebration arranged by the Junior synagogue.

THE HIGH HOLY DAYS

The value of the Rosh ha-Shanah and Yom Kippur holy days is indicated in the course of the considerations presented in the chapter on Formal Worship.

The following suggestions may prove helpful:

Refreshments are an important element in all celebrations. Let them consist of items traditionally associated with the festival or holiday. Candies or desserts in which matzoh meal is an ingredient, are associated with Passover. Blintzes and kreplach are Shabuot delicacies. The hamantashen and Purim are inseparable. Potato pancakes or *latkes* for Hanukkah. Figs and dates on Hamisha Asar Beshvat. Taglach and Floden are usually associated with Sukkot.

The musical selections for community singing vary also in content from festival to festival. The song books published by Israel Goldfarb, Young Judea, The Jewish Welfare Board, and others offer a wide range of choice. A fertile field for such selections can be found in the early Yiddish operettas of the Goldfaden period. Compositions of Binder will also prove helpful.

Games are especially useful in individual club celebrations. Some of the festivals are associated with special games. Nuts constitute the implements of a number of Passover indoor games. A dreidel is universally asso-

ciated with Hanukkah. Young Judea, the Associated
Talmud Torahs of Philadelphia, the Bureau of Jewish
Education in Chicago have published collections of suitable games for festivals and other occasions. It is possible also to modify the general games in such a way as
to give them Jewish meaning and content. The collections of Bancroft and "Phunology", or "Good Times
for All Times" are typical of the books useful for this
purpose.

Pageantry and dramatic presentations are very
fruitful forms of festival celebrations. They provide
opportunities for the exercise of many abilities in
drama, music, literature, and arts and crafts. The children entrusted with the various arrangements have an
opportunity to exercise administrative ability as well
as leadership. In the individual club celebrations, opportunities may also be given for the writing and production of original plays and pageants. The Junior
Synagogue had best use professionally produced material.

In deciding on the play or pageant to be presented,
it is well to bear in mind that the plot of the play need
not be the original historic event which the festival celebrates. Jewish history provides a large number of happenings which are in harmony with the festival or tend
to bring out its meaning. Thus the Jews have lived
through many a crisis similar to that of Purim. In fact,
many a community in commemoration of some experience has observed a local annual Purim for a great many
years. Similarly, there are events indicating Jewish capacity to sacrifice for religious institutions.

The exodus from Egypt is not the only time when
a great many of our people were freed from bondage,

and the establishing of great educational institutions adequately represents the spirit of the Festival of Sha-buot.

In their original creations the boys and girls should be encouraged to try to understand the spirit of each festival, and to multiply the forms in which that spirit could be expressed.

TOPICS FOR DISCUSSION

1. Are there any problems in the modern world to which specific ideals associated with the Jewish festivals are applicable? Can the ideals associated with the various festivals be helpful in solving them?

2. Consider directions for several parlor and outdoor games taken from some general book on games, such as Bancroft. How could the terminology and the directions for the playing of these games be changed as to make them suitable for a festival celebration?

3. What local, national, and international Jewish and non-Jewish institutions may be associated with each festival? Discuss the reasons for such association.

REFERENCES

Greenstone, J. H. *The Jewish Religion.* Pages 24-34, 46-48, 57-59, 60-67, 74-114, 122-130.

Eisenstein, Ira. *What We Mean by Religion.* Pages 66-135.

Hayyim Schauss, The Jewish Festivals. Pages 5-12, 27-30, 43-46, 65-76, 88-95, 174-186, 189-207, 228-236, 252-271.

CHAPTER VI

INFORMAL WORSHIP

Many people perform religious ceremonials and observances for no other reason than that they are part of a religious code. They are rules that must be obeyed as evidence of yielding to Divine authority. They possess other values, however, that can be demonstrated in reason. Ceremonials are the language of feeling and aspiration. They are acts expressing emotions, hopes and desires, and stimulating the deeds through which these aspirations may be attained. We clasp hands to express good will and friendship. When the handshake is hearty, it will make for a greater readiness to behave in a friendly manner. Primitive peoples will execute a war, hunt, or fishing, dance before embarking on these enterprises. The performance of the ceremony prepares the group at least psychologically for the execution of the undertaking.

If there were no ceremonies, feelings and aspirations would remain vague, and lack purposeful crystallization. If ceremonies are not followed by activities in real life, they tend to encase the individual in a dream world moving from feeling to feeling, from wish to hope, without the possibility of realization of aim and ideal.

There are ceremonies that perform still another function. They add an element of higher aspiration to the feeling they express. If all that is desired is a sign of friendship, a handshake will suffice. When the friendship takes on a more intimate character, partaking of food together will prove adequate. It is possible also that the friendship may be based on the sharing of a task making for an increase in human happiness. In such a case other elements are added to the ceremony which gives it a distinct character. Insofar as it is related to the reaching out for the higher life it partakes of the nature of worship.

Synagogue life offers a plenitude of ceremony and observances which may be made meaningful and helpful to the adolescent through the club. In addition, new ceremonies may be provided to express the feelings of the boy or girl on certain important occasions in their lives.

I.

The first series of ceremonials to be considered have to do with the entrance of new members to the adolescent organization and graduation of the members of the Junior Synagogue into the Young People's League.

a. All boys who attain the age of 13 and the girls who attain the age of 12 should be formally inducted into the Junior Synagogue by special ceremony. If enough boys and girls become Bar or Bas Mitzvah, to form two new groups, the clubs may be initiated as such, otherwise there should be an initiation of the individuals into the club nearest their ages. Ceremonies of initiation may take various forms. The following synopsis is given only by way of suggestion:

The numbers to be initiated are gathered outside of the meeting room. A member of the initiating team is with them and acts as the guide and mentor. He knocks on the door six times. In response to "Who is there?" he explains that a number of neophytes are ready to enter Jewish life and want the privilege of affiliating with the Junior Synagogue as the pathway through which there may open to them the privilege of Jewish living. The door opens. A spotlight plays upon the captain of the initiating team. In his introductory remarks he explains that the Junior Synagogue is a fellowship through which, by friendship and cooperation, the individuals will be led to appreciate and to enjoy the blessings of Jewish life. The Junior Synagogue will open to the candidates the portals of the present day Jewish world, will help strengthen the kinship between them and the great men and women that have expressed the highest and holiest in Jewish life in the past, and will reveal to them the great aspirations of the Jewish people for a future of happiness for humanity as a whole. The leader then conducts the neophytes to various parts of the room where a representative dwells for a few minutes on the different aspects of the initiation. At the conclusion there is a summary by the leader; the initiated group is then asked whether they are willing to enter into the life of the Junior Synagogue for the purpose of participating in Jewish life as a whole. Upon their affirmative response, they are installed as a club member of the Junior Synagogue and receive the blessing of the Rabbi.

b. Some clubs receive applications of individuals during the course of the year. These individuals may be boys or girls who have not had the benefit of training in the religious school of the congregation, and while supported by some members of the club, there may be a question as to whether they would fit in with the life of the club. An initiation providing an experience that would in a way set their thoughts and hearts in the right direction, would be helpful. The following plan has proven successful in a number of instances. Other plans may be thought of.

The member to be initiated, after filling out the application and being passed upon by the membership committee, is invited to attend a meeting of the club. As far as he is concerned, it is a regular meeting. The business of the meeting is passed through rapidly until there comes the report of the last fund-raising activity. This is the beginning of the initiation. A member rises and explains that there were $15.00 realized. The report is accepted, and another member rises and moves that the money be divided as follows: One-half should be contributed to some philanthropic national cause, 25% to be devoted to the refreshments of the next festival celebration, and the balance to remain in the treasury. The motion is seconded. A member rises and offers an amendment that a moving picture party be arranged for, and the money be used to pay for the tickets and refreshments to follow. Discussion follows. In the course of the discussion, which grows more and more heated, the following points are made:

1. The object of the Junior Synagogue is to assume responsibility for Jewish life to the extent of our powers. The money obtained should accordingly be utilized in such a way as to indicate our interest in the various Jewish causes.

2. The objectives of the Junior Synagogue as preached by the Rabbi are uninteresting and dull. The money raised came in as a result of the hard work of the members selling tickets and in preparing for the event,

etc. They have a right to use it as they please, and should have good times with it so that belonging to the Junior Synagogue may be a real source of pleasure.

3. There is pleasure to be obtained in good works and in the friendship and social life resulting from the work done together. We not only want to have a good time but we also want to do those things that will enable many individuals, Jews and non-Jews, to enjoy life. Our own happiness is incomplete when we don't do our share to increase the happiness of others.

4. This is "sissy" talk and preaching, of which we get enough in the synagogue. If we want to be grown-up men and women, we ought to take care of ourselves first.

The discussion waxes hot and finally results in a split of the group. A number go to one end of the room, talking amongst themselves, another group at another end of the room, leaving the one to be initiated by himself. After a minute, one member comes to him and says: "You can see the kind of a crowd we have here. Those other fellows don't know what the club ought to be like. We have decided to get out of the Junior Synagogue so that we can have a club and have real good times. Will you join us?" If the answer is, "I don't think I want to join you, I want to look into the matter further," the word is passed that the neophyte has passed the initiation. He is congratulated upon his understanding of the higher values and is formally accepted as a member of the club. If, however, he says "Fine, I will join you," the meeting is immediately reconvened and the report is made in his presence that he has failed. The motion is made that he be rejected. A member rises to speak against the motion. The test was too hard. The one to be initiated was led astray by the fact that so many of the group took the wrong position. As soon as he is in the club and realizes the depth of their happiness and the richness of their social life, he will understand the value of the activities of the club. If he shows any form of realization as to the meaning of the Junior Synagogue he is formally accepted as a member.

In both forms of initiation there ought to be an adequate song to conclude the ceremonies. In fact, music can play a great part in the first form of initiation. It would be well for the members of the class to endeavor to write up the text for these initiations.

c. The initiation of the older boys and girls into the Young People's League should be developed by the League. The Junior Synagogue as a whole, however, may develop a farewell ceremony in which the following thoughts should be expressed:

1. A sense of congratulation upon their entering the larger field of Jewish activity.

2. Confidence in the continuation of their interest and friendship in the Junior Synagogue. The event should partake of the nature of a social.

II.

The club meetings need not open or close with a ceremonial. They come frequently, and the feeling they engender is of a convivial nature and does not require any special ceremony. The monthly meetings of the Junior Synagogue, however, do warrant an opening prayer. They embrace all the clubs, and take on a different meaning. The prayer however does not necessarily have to be addressed directly to God. When the name "God" is used too often and the prayers become a pure matter of form, all meaning is dried out of it.

A statement like: "We have gathered again for the purpose of taking counsel as to how we can advance Jewish life, deepen the friendships that exist amongst us and enlarge the extent of our cooperation" would be appropriate. For every meeting there ought to be added a few sentences or a paragraph referring to the exact purpose of the meeting. Perhaps different members should be appointed to write these invocations. If they are not sanctimonious and stereotyped, they may prove effective.

The opening and closing meetings of the year, however, may include a special prayer expressing the sentiments appropriate to the occasion. Under all circumstances it is best that the prayers are not stereotyped, and are written by the members. There are other occasions when more formal worship ceremonies are in place.

1. The illness of any member of the club should be noted, and prayers for his recovery recited. It is customary also to recite a number of psalms as a means of attuning one's heart and mind to a higher plane before uttering the prayer. There is great value in this ceremony. If the illness is not contagious, a committee may be appointed to visit the member and express the good wishes of his fellow members. In any event, some gift of flowers with an appropriate card may be sent. If the illness of the child takes a serious turn, the Junior Synagogue offers a prayer and expresses its good wishes to the boy or girl and his family.

2. The heart of the festival celebration is the spiritual aspiration it represents. The reasons the Jewish festivals survived are not contained in the mere fact that

they commemorate a phase of Jewish life in the past. They have present value in the form of socialized action and feeling they foster. To bring out this vital element of the festival, it would be well that at every celebration some ceremonial indicate interest in an appropriate social, educational, or welfare cause. This is best done by the Junior Synagogue rather than by the club, and representatives of the adolescents and of the local adult leaders of the cause or movement should participate in the ceremony.

The cause chosen should be harmonious with the spirit of the festival. At Sukkot, for instance, the emphasis should be on welfare activities. The religious ceremonials of the festival are favorable to the strengthening of the desire to share. It may be well to adopt a rule that one-tenth of the annual income of the Junior Synagogue should be given at the festival celebration, to one or more organizations created for the relief of the poor and underprivileged. The pledge is made during the celebration. The adult representatives of the Federation or welfare institutions acknowledge the pledge.

Thanksgiving Day is a suitable time for indicating our ties with our non-Jewish fellow Americans through joint Thanksgiving services for the blessings that all of us have found in this great country.

At Hanukkah there may be a token of the interest in the Synagogue. The Junior Synagogue may buy something for the Synagogue library, add to the prayer books, Bible, or make a presentation for the further beautifying of the Synagogue. If the adolescents also have some children in the field of arts and crafts, the presentation may be a product of their creative talents.

Hamisha Asar Beshvat should be a time when the

ties of the group with Palestine are emphasized. This ought to take the form of a token sacrifice for the Palestinian Institution—the planting of trees, the work of Hadassah, such as the kindergarten lunches, penny luncheon fund, medical service, etc., are suitable objectives.

Purim is essentially the festival expressing the unity of Israel. At that time there should take place an appropriate expression of interest in the United Jewish Campaigns, the Ort, Hias, etc. There may also be an announcement of an interchange of gifts with a school, class or club in other lands.

During the Passover it is well to express love of liberty, equality and democracy not only with reference to the Jew but also the non-Jew. Our joy at being freed from Egyptian bondage is best expressed in freeing others from similar enslavement and deprivation.

The seminaries and national congregational and religious educational organizations come to our mind when we think of the associations with Shabuot.

It is through these organizations that we maintain today our covenant to further Jewish life and ideals.

TOPICS FOR DISCUSSION

1. What other occasion in connection with club activities or events in the life of the members would worship exercises be appropriate? Suggest appropriate exercises.

2. Some of the exercises suggested in this chapter are generally denominated worship. Others are not. Is the author right in regarding them all as in the category of worship? Discuss fully.

REFERENCES

Dimock, Hedley S. *Rediscovering the Adolescent.* Pages 152-170.

Greenstone, J. H. *The Jewish Religion.* Pages 159-167, 243-297.

Singer Prayer Book. Pages 278-298, 300-304, 310-312, 314-317, 322-325.

CHAPTER VII

FORMAL WORSHIP

Regular worship exercises, daily, Sabbath and festival, conducted in the synagogue as a rule, are usually termed "services". This is rather unfortunate as it conveys a wrong idea of the purpose of these exercises. It gives the impression that the pageantry, chants and prayers in some mysterious way supply a need of the Divine, in return for which the wishes and desires of the worshiper are granted. This anthropomorphic conception of the Divine can do naught but harm. In times past, the priests who conducted the ceremony in connection with the Temple exercises, really expended much energy. They served the people of Israel, and their efforts could well be called "Services." The present-day rabbi or cantor who leads the exercises, may also be said to serve—his people. From the standpoint of the congregation, however, the ceremonies are engaged in for the purpose of satisfying real needs, in the process of building Jewish character and raising personality to higher planes of feeling, thinking and living.

It is not easy to be a Jew. Apart from the discriminations and persecutions there is a difficulty even more taxing. The centrifugal forces of appetite, desire and

narrow social outlook divide the personality and prevent wholehearted acceptance of the higher integrating
and socializing aims as the dominant and ultimate end
of our lives and institutions. It is hard to rise to a spiritual plane of living, fully inspired by the sense of the
brotherhood of man, the corollary of the Fatherhood
of God. The humanly conceived institutions ordering
our lives, our families, clubs, business organizations,
communities, and the political entities—city, country,
state and nation—are not always effective in making
for a higher degree of human kinship. They often constitute disruptive forces, perverting and preventing integrated personality. Efforts at being kind, generous
and loving are often rewarded with betrayal, deprivation and persecution.

The narrow personal needs and appetites are re-
sponded to despite a knowledge of the higher demands
of society and personality. When the act of commission
or omission is over there is regret which may take on a
very painful character. This remorse is not always
helpful. The consciousness that one has failed in high
purpose can act as a bar to other attempts. The conviction may develop that one is by nature too weak to
live in accordance with the difficult standards necessary
for the good life.

What can be done to recreate our spiritual aspirations? How can one experience the sense of kinship with
fellow human beings who are similarly dedicated to the
increase of life and happiness? It is the need of drawing
nearer to the Divine that was served by the ceremonies
attending the ancient offering of sacrifices, and it is the
same necessity that is satisfied through Synagogue worship.

What is the character of Jewish worship—and how does it raise the participant to a higher level of existence?

1. Jewish worship tends to permeate every phase of life. It is as though the lines of demarcation between the secular and the holy have been moved forward to sanctify more and more of life's areas. Benedictions accompany, precede or follow many an act or transaction in which human beings engage; for instance: on awakening from sleep, the ancient Jew recites "Blessed art Thou, O Lord, our God, King of the Universe, who openest the eyes of the blind." On dressing himself, he recited, "Blessed art Thou, O Lord, our God, King of the Universe, who clothest the naked." On tying the girdle about him he recited, "Blessed art Thou, O Lord, our God, King of the Universe, who girdest Israel with strength".

It is interesting to note how the benediction helps to point to a larger and more socialized aspect of human or Jewish interests. God is thanked not so much for what the individual is able to achieve, but more for what Israel or humanity accomplished.

There is grace before and after meals. There are services on dedicating a new home or entering the house or leaving for a long journey or returning from one, or on recovery from illness. Every unusual natural phenomenon, such as lightning, thunder, the rainbow—even the meeting with a great man—evokes a benediction.

Certain acts in life themselves become acts of worship. Partaking of food is made a sacred act when the object is to gain strength for worthful living. To emphasize the sacred character of the repast it is enjoined that when two or more eat at one board the table talk should contain also words of "Torah". Covering one's head is a sign of reverence and humility. This is why all acts of worship have from the distant past been observed with covered head. It is proper, however, that one should be always conscious of the Kingdom of Heaven. Accordingly, great Rabbis in the past would keep their heads covered while outside the home. Nowadays, Orthodox Jews wear their hats at all times and places.

2. Education, teaching and studying the Torah, are holy occupations and are included in the category of worship experience. The heart of the ancient festival celebrations was the instruction of adult and child in the ways of godly living. The Bet ha-Midrash, the house of study, is regarded as holier than the synagogue and it is more meritorious to pray therein. It has been customary from ancient days to precede or follow a synagogue service with a lesson in the Mishnah, Talmud or Bible. Some parts of the morning services are purely of an educational nature. Studying the Torah has been prescribed as efficacious in alleviating physical illness and other troubles. It is a direct means for achieving communion with the Divine.

Jewish educational matter is not limited to the Bible, Talmud or rabbinic readings. Principles of action that may affect one's physical life; laws and forms covering human relationships, are also included in the codes of religious law, compiled by the great Jewish authorities. If a distinction is made at all between secular and religious educational material, it is in the purpose for which the material is studied. If the objective is holy, if it is to help bring nearer the establishment of the Kingdom of God, the matter is sacred.

3. The greater part by far of the synagogue services

is communal rather than individual in nature. The worshiper addresses himself to his Father in Heaven, but he does not speak as an individual. He thinks of himself as a member of the House of Israel or of humanity. It is more meritorious to pray with nine others than to pray by one's self. The set prayers, however, are the same for the individual as for the congregation. They are expressions of congregational, communal, and national feelings, needs and aspirations. It is better to worship as part of a congregation, because then one feels himself more readily a part of the community of Israel.

There is present, too, the sense of responsibility for the moral shortcomings of the brethren of the worshiper. Prayers of penitence are in the plural. "Forgive us for the sin which we have committeed" is the constant refrain in the penitential passages. He not only prays for others who have sinned, but regards himself a sinner because of their transgressions. Salvation, too, is not an individual aspiration. It is purely social and human. Not even Israel will be saved alone. Three times a day the Jews pray, "We therefore hope in Thee, O Lord(our God . . . when the world will be perfected under the Kingdom of the Almighty, and all the children of flesh will call upon Thy name, when Thou wilt turn unto Thyself all the wicked of the earth . . . For the Kingdom is Thine, and to all eternity Thou wilt reign in glory; as it is written in Thy Torah: The Lord shall reign for ever and ever. And it is said, "And the Lord shall be King over all the earth; in that day shall the Lord be One and His name One".

4. There is identification not only with the community of Israel but also with Israel's past generations. The Bible commands that the pascal lamb be eaten while the

worshipper is attired in the same way as his ancestors were during the exodus from Egypt. The Israelite is commanded to dwell in the sukkah because his ancestors lived in booths while wandering through the desert. An important part of the liturgy of the Day of Atonement consists of a dramatic recital of the sacrifical ceremonies observed by the High Priest and the people during the days of the Temple.

What ever else the ceremonies consist of, there is usually included the bringing into the present the thoughts and feelings experienced by the ancestors in the past. Events in Jewish history that are in harmony with the feeling-tone of the festival become associated with it, and achieve an addition or modification of the liturgy or ceremonial. The present generation, then, participating in the festival service, finds the holy day feeling-tone enriched by harmonious overtones—echoes of the ages. There are answering chords in the Jewish heart and soul.

5. While worship in the synagogue is primarily an esthetic experience with song and procession, it is bound up with life. The quality of life in the community affects it, and in return it stimulates the individual to sacrifice for social causes. In the not distant past it was customary and regarded as proper for an individual to interrupt the services in the synagogue if he felt himself treated unjustly by the community or by a fellow-worshipper. In many congregations it is the practice to announce donations to the synagogue, the school, the hospital and other social institutions, during the service. In some synagogues this is done during intermissions in the reading of the Torah—in others, after the Torah is restored to the Ark.

6. The Jewish prayer book consists for the most part

of set prayers. There is very little opportunity for spontaneous prayer. Great events affecting large numbers of the Jewish people have resulted in additions to the prayer book. There have been growth and development, but owing to the feeling that worship should be communal there is a far greater tendency towards uniformity in the Jewish ritual than in many others. The fact must be noted, however, that in the past the liturgy admitted of additions and modifications.

The worship needs of the adolescent differ in a number of important details from those of the adult. Much of our sense of sin and culpability comes from acts or deeds which involve money or property rights. The boy or girl, however, cannot experience the realities of situations underlying such acts because he does not need money or property, or the commodities for which these are necessary, in the same way that the adult does. His needs are provided for by his parents or guardians—his world is sheltered; his temptations are in the domain of his appetites and desire for freedom of action or for power, which are more circumscribed in the adolescent than in the adult. It is doubtful, too, whether he can envisage the world and the actions and reactions of its social component elements in the same way that the grown-up does.

The prayer book and the adult ritual of worship do not answer as a whole to his worship needs. When, in response to pressure on the part of teachers and parents, boys and girls participate in adult worship, even when the exercises are conducted by themselves, they are not undergoing a satisfactory, or a satisfying worship experience.

Yet there are many elements in the make-up of the growing boy and girl which reach out to the elements in adult worship. The adolescent can become indignant at ingratitude, injustice or persecution even when he personally has no experience of the same. He can sympathize with the victim. He can form ideals and dedicate his life to them. He can admire and revere men and women who have sacrificed for similiar ideals.

The adolescent accordingly can find a spiritual satisfaction in the feeling that he is cooperating with the great souls of Israel's past, and the great personalities of Israel's present. He can share their aspirations, take pride in their achievements, and strengthen his resolutions to follow the paths blazed by them.

The adolescent knows what temptation is, though the areas in which he may be tempted are more or less limited. He can suffer remorse, and he has need of exercises that will free him from the feeling that because he has failed once or several times success is impossible for him. He can sense also the challenge to his ideals in the life about him, and he has need of acquiring increase of spiritual strength from the immersion of his self in the thoughts and feelings of the worship exercised.

There are many elements in the liturgy that respond to these needs. The reading of the Torah, for instance, and the pageantry associated with it, are important for the purpose of expressing the loyalty to Judaism, its Torah, and the value of its historic continuity. When the portion read is translated, and its relevance to present-day problems is explained through homily and sermon, there is a deeper realization of the guidance received from the passages read, and their interpretation in the sermon. The Sh'ma and the selections preceding and following it express Israel's devotion to its God and faith.

The introductory hymns help to strengthen the sense of unity with Israel's past when it is understood that in their recital there is dramatization of Temple worship.

To make these elements of the prayer book meaningful, the club program should include activities through which the way they can function may become evident, and the needs which they satisfy should be brought to the surface of consciousness. In other words, there must develop a full need for worship, and an understanding and a realization of how the various parts of the prayer book can be utilized in such a way as to answer these needs.

What specifically can be done through the club program?

1. The informal worship activities, the exercises at the opening and closing of the year's work, at the opening of the monthly meetings of the Junior Synagogue, the reverent periods during certain elements of the festival celebrations, the forms through which the members express their concern when a fellow member is ill, etc., etc.—all tend to make the members familiar with attitudes in the domain of worship. The boys and girls will also sense the value of these attitudes.

2. The worship exercises should entail participation of many of the children. Those who have good voices lead in the congregational singing and chant the more difficult selections. The service itself is divided in a number of parts, and different children conduct each part. Different children may read the portion of the Torah together with the translation, may deliver the sermonette, and may recite or sing the original prayers. This participation is helpful in evoking and maintaining interest in the exercises.

3. No element of the worship exercises should be introduced without a preparatory period during which the necessity and value of that element should be made evident. For instance, the reading of the Torah and the pageantry in connection with taking the Scroll out of the Ark and returning it, are significant ceremonies expressing the devotion, reverence and loyalty to the Jewish sacred law. The Sh'ma expresses loyalty to our faith. These meanings of the above mentioned ceremonies will be accepted by the children as perfectly natural and proper, since they understand that the Junior Synagogue as a whole exists for the purpose of enabling them to participate more and more in Jewish life. Similarly, the emotional significance of every ceremony, every prayer, should be made clear in advance, and the feelings the ceremony expresses should be evoked through an adequate presentation and discussion.

4. The worship exercises should be bound up with the interests and feelings of the children as they develop in the club activity. Several examples will make this clear.

(a) Current events evoking strong feelings in the hearts of the children are discussed at the meetings of the clubs or the Junior Synagogue, and their implication for adequate attitudes crystallized. The accounts in the press of Palestinian events, for instance, stimulate decisive phases of Zionist activity the subject of discussion, oration and drama. It then becomes a simple matter to direct attention to certain fundamental problems. What shall be our goal—cooperation or competition—friendship or victory? If the former, shall we express our hopes and aspirations through poem or prayer, to be included at an appropriate point in the services? Have our ancestors expressed similar aspirations? Shall we recite what they said? During what part of the service shall we participate in these special exercises? Who shall be appointed to write the poem or prayer?

(b) The festivals derive their value not only from the association with the season and with certain phases of Jewish history, but also from their significance for present-day attitude and action. This is reflected in the program of the festival celebrations. It should also be reflected in the formal worship. Just as actual happenings tend to evoke moods and feelings which may lead to appropriate action, so will the feelings evoked by the festival worship influence the attitudes of the children to the world about them. Shabuot, for instance, associated as it is with the concept of the covenant and the source of Jewish learning, will help focus attention on institutions of higher Jewish learning—their problems and aspirations. This interest will in turn reflect itself in the club program.

(c) The life of clubs and of the Junior Synagogue offers many opportunities for crystallizing and expressing worship attitudes that will help raise the life of the boy or girl to higher levels. Elections, competitive events, integration in some larger congregational or communal activity, naturally evokes the feelings and aspirations which can be given a directive tendency through embodiment in special worship exercises made part of the regular ceremonies.

When shall the regular worship exercises take place? It depends upon the training the boys and girls have had before entering the Junior Synagogue. Where the school has instituted children's Sabbath morning exer-

cises and had organized and conducted them in such a
way as to give the pupils satisfying worship experiences,
the Junior Synagogue may continue to conduct these
exercises. If, however, that has not been done, and the
Junior Synagogue has to start from the beginning, it
may be well to commence with the Sabbath afternoon
worship. Under all circumstances there should be special
worship periods arranged for the high Holy Days.
Rabbi Silverman's "Junior Prayer Book" is suitable for
the Sabbath and festivals. For the High Holy Day services, either Rabbi Rose's book or Rabbi Silverman's is
adequate.

TOPICS FOR DISCUSSION

1. What selection in the Daily and Sabbath Prayer
books can be helpful in meeting the common problems of
the adolescent?

2. What selection in the Festival and High Holiday
Prayer Book can be helpful in meeting the common
problems of the adolescent?

3. Rivalry for an office in the Junior Synagogue runs
very high. There is much personal feeling. Plan a worship exercise that would help.

REFERENCES

Eisenstein, Ira. *What We Mean by Religion*. Pages 11-14,
1-25.

Greenstone, J. H. *The Jewish Religion*. Pages 134-142, 145-
157.

CHAPTER VIII

THE CLUB PROGRAM

The threads of our various discussions can now be drawn together to help define the outline of an adequate program of Junior adolescent activities.

There are two fundamental conditions the proposed program must meet. It must make for increasing participation by the members in Jewish adult institutions and movements as their powers for such participation grows; and it must utilize the aptitudes and capacities and interests of the children. The institutions and movements have various aims and purposes; the participation of the boys and girls should be motivated by their acceptance of these ends. Among these ideas there is the religious one. It seeks the increase of life and happiness. This ideal constitutes a norm for evaluating all institutions and movements. The institution devoted to the fostering of the religious ideals is the synagogue and participation in some of its activities will tend to give a unifying meaning to all their efforts and interests, and aid in the growth and integration of their personalities.

The members' aptitudes and capacities are as a rule expressed in a number of well defined patterns of activity, namely, leadership, administration, literature, drama, music, dance, arts and crafts, and athletics.

The program should provide activities in these areas based upon what the aptitudes of the boys and girls may happen to be. These activities should be purposeful, however, in the sense that the participants know and accept as desirable the objectives of these elements of the program. The activities may serve a variety of purposes, and several activities may combine to serve one purpose. It may be well at this point to indicate how the different activities can be utilized for ends within the purview of the Junior Synagogue.

Leadership

Members who have this capacity can occupy positions of authority in the Junior Synagogue, the constituent clubs, or the various standing and special committees. As a rule, their abilities will be recognized, and they will be elected or appointed to the various offices by the children themselves. It is best that there be no interference on the part of the club leader even when in his judgment a mistake is about to be made. If the larger purposes of the Junior Synagogue are adequately kept in the forefront, rivalry will be robbed of its injurious effects. A proviso in the Constitution that nobody may hold an office for more than two consecutive terms will prevent mistakes from doing too much harm.

The objective of leadership activities is obvious—to bring nearer the realization of the purposes of the organization.

These vary from building up adequate teams for competitive events, to heading the Junior Synagogue as a whole.

The relationship of the various purposes to each other and to the higher objectives of the organization, can be kept in mind by the club leader and clarified to the children from time to time through the agencies best adapted for such a purpose—namely, the periodical, the club meetings, worship exercises, etc.

Administration

The secretaries, recording, financial, correspondence, the managers of the teams, the chairmen of the fund-raising functions, etc. are drawn from among the boys or girls possessing administrative talents.

Here, too, the appointments or elections are in the hands of the members. When responsibility has been placed, the club leader should give every possible aid to the boy or girl, so as to enable him to carry out his duties adequately. The failure of the boy or girl will not only affect his own social growth, but may also hurt the club as a whole. Many a club leader, however, makes the mistake of actually doing the work of the officer for him. If the boy or girl lacks the abilities an officer requires, he should realize it as soon as possible so that he may devote himself to the type of work for which he is better fitted. The leader should see that the member understands that his importance is not measured by the office or form of activity but rather by the whole-heartedness of his devotion and service.

Literature

Literary aptitudes find expression in a number of directions. Original essays, short stories, poems and orations are part of the regular club program, and the best efforts in this direction can be used in the monthly program of the Junior Synagogue. The club may have a periodical of its own, which is read at every meeting or at alternate meetings. This paper also contains write-ups of the club news, occasional personal notes, special articles on timely topics for the children, editorials and news of the congregation's activities that interest its boys and girls.

The members with literary ability write the special prayers for the various occasions which are to be incorporated in the worship exercises. They contribute members to the debating team, able to organize and write up the presentation of their respective sides in the debate.

The objectives of these activities are obvious. They enrich the club and Junior Synagogue programs; they constitute part of the festival celebrations; and they clarify and carry forward the Junior Synagogue's social service and religious objectives.

The various committees for cooperation with other Jewish and non-Jewish institutions and movements may use the periodical for educational purposes in regard to these institutions and for the dissemination of news about them, as well as for officially recording their findings and doings.

Dramatics

The members who have dramatic ability may express it through recitations, orations, participation in pantomime, dialogue, skits and plays. They may also take part in debates. If any member evidences ability to write plays or dialogues, opportunities may be found for the utilization of his efforts.

Members with dramatic talent contribute to club programs, monthly programs of the Junior Synagogue and festival celebrations. Purim is a time particularly suitable for acting and dramatics.

The work of many important institutions and movements can be brought out through dramatic presentation and pageantry. The persecutions of the Jews in Germany and Eastern Europe, for instance, can be depicted through pageant and drama, pantomime and the radio dramatic technique. Jewish March of Time, radio presentations of "This Month in Jewish History," make vivid important current and historic events. Such presentations are useful preparatory steps in stimulating the Junior Synagogue to adequate sacrifice, and for stimulating interest in further study and research, the dramatic talent of the Junior Synagogue can be used also for direct aid to these institutions and causes. Admission fees may be charged and the funds thus raised used for the benefit of the cause.

Music

Vocal and instrumental music numbers constitute important elements in the programs of the individual club as well as of the Junior Synagogue. There may be built up also group organizations, choral or instrumental ensembles, if enough talent is available. At times the children with musical ability join with those interested in dramatics to produce pageants, operettas and music drama.

The children with musical ability contribute to the inspirational value of the worship exercises. They provide cantors and the choir to lead in congregational singing, or render more elaborate renditions of the prayers. They may also arrange concerts of Jewish music of various forms—religious, folk, national, etc. These recitals may be given for purely educational purposes or as fund-raising enterprises for various worthwhile causes.

Arts and Crafts

Many aptitudes are included under the term "Arts and Crafts," and they can all help to enrich the club or the Junior Synagogue program. The club journal is specially bound and illustrated by the members who have talents in those directions. The gavel and other appurtenances of the club can be made by the boys and girls. The walls ,too, may be decorated by them. If the club has many members who possess the necessary ability, articles both useful and ornamental can be made for the home. At the proper time they can be presented to the families of each club member.

The Junior Synagogue can be similarly benefited by the children gifted in this field. They paint the scenes, decorations and curtains for the dramatic productions and pageants. They make the gavel and decorate the walls of the meeting room. The Junior Synagogue may desire to send gifts to children in Palestine or other lands. Nothing is so satisfying to giver and receiver as articles made by the children themselves. On the proper occasion, gifts can be presented to the synagogue. The ceremonial objects made by the club members possessing the necessary skill are very acceptable.

Dance

Some of the members may have ability in the field of aesthetic and dramatic dance or pantomime. It is well to recognize these abilities and to use them in the pageant or pantomime for the purpose of enriching the dramatic and musical elements of the program.

Athletics

Adolescents are particularly interested in athletics. Practically every member of every club is desirous of participating in one or more different games; track, baseball, basketball, football, tennis, wrestling, boxing, etc., are popular at different seasons, and time should be provided for the chidren to participate in them. Those who evidence superior ability form teams that represent the club or Junior Synagogue. They are also used for fund-raising purposes.

The Lag-Ba-Omer festival is usually observed, in part, through athletic contests.

TOPICS FOR DISCUSSION

1. Indicate the vocational significance of this chapter.

2. What are the types of club leaders required for the proper functioning of a Junior Synagogue?

REFERENCE

Dimock, Hedley S. *Rediscovering the Adolescent.* Pages 171-204.

CHAPTER IX

THE CLUB PROGRAM
(CONTINUED)

The former chapter has outlined the ways in which the various abilities of the members may find useful and purposeful expression. This should not be taken to mean that a member's interest is generally in the activity itself and that the object and end of the activity is the concern only of the adult and the club leader. As a matter of fact, mere action without purpose is not satisfying to human beings. What is uppermost in the minds of the boys and girls are aims and purposes. The ball is thrown not to exercise the muscles, but to make a higher score, to win, to establish a record. The race is run not to expend surplus energy, but to get ahead, to merit admiration and applause.

The objectives of the Junior Synagogue must be accepted by the members, they must be their very own. The presentation of the cause or institution which they are asked to advance, may be cogent and appealing, but if this is the main motivating element, it does not suffice. The aims must find a dominant position in the ongoing stream of the achieving and striving that is the very essence of their lives.

The projects of the club arise out of the situations in

which the club and the members find themselves. What the synagogue contributes to the development and growth of the personalities of the members is an environment presenting a succession of situations that demand responses in the forms of activities of the Junior Synagogue. Some of these situations consist of the inter-relationships existing among the members of the club, others derive their meaning from the relationship of the club to other clubs. The position of the club as a constituent member of the Junior Congregation is an element contributing purpose and aim to their life. The adult world, especially the adult Jewish world, affects them through their connections with the Young People's League of the Congregation and through relationships of the Junior Synagogue with adult movements and institutions.

A

Instances of projects developing out of club interests are the following:

1.

The club decides to act as a host to another club of the same or opposite sex. The club accepts an invitation to be the guests of another club. In either event it prepares a program for the purpose of entertaining the guest club or of contributing to the program of the host. One or two meetings preceding the events are given over, in whole or in part, to rehearsals of its share in the program.

The program committee decides on the numbers to be contributed, bearing in mind the talents of the children, and one or more meetings are devoted to the rehearsals.

2.

The club is permitted to provide the whole program for the regular monthly meeting of the Junior Synagogue.

The numbers usually include at least one element of major interest, such as a dramatic sketch, a debate, and several vocal numbers or instrumental selections, depending upon the talents of the members. Here, too, a preliminary meeting or, if need be, several such meetings are devoted to rehearsals.

3.

The club is challenged by another club to a debate, or a literary contest. In order that a club may put its best foot forward, as it were, an elimination contest is held which together with a rehearsal for the principal event, occupies one or several club meetings.

4.

The club decides to invite the parents of the children to a party, and prepares a program for them. The club accepts the invitation of the parents to a party, and decides to make a contribution to the program. The procedure is the same as if another club is the host or guest. Several meetings are similarly occupied in rehearsals and preparations.

5.

The club engages in a fund-raising effort in connection with which entertainment is felt to be desirable. Again the program committee decides on the numbers, and one or more meetings are devoted to rehearsals.

B

The following are instances of projects arising out of the relationship between the club and the Junior Synagogue:

1.

The Junior Synagogue decides on a study of the work of some institution or organization devoted to Jewish or humanitarian purposes. If a member of a club has a share in this work, he reports to the club on what he or his committee has found, before reporting to the Junior Synagogue as a whole. This strengthens the interest of one or more clubs in the project.

2.

In connection with the worship exercises, a member of the club may be appointed to render a solo. If it is of a suitable nature, he may be asked to sing for fellow members of the club as part of the program.

3.

The Junior Synagogue may decide that problems have arisen in the area of individual or interclub relationship. The council feels that if these problems will be clarified by formal discussion on the subject by the members of a particular club or clubs, it accordingly asks each of the clubs to make this topic an important part of one of its programs. The discussions may be conducted by a leader, and guided by a syllabus.

4.

Worship exercises may be made more meaningful and helpful when the participants feel deeply the difficulties

and perplexities in which the exercises are intended to
be helpful. This is equally true when the subject of the
exercises be some present-day social or personal problem. The Junior Synagogue may therefore arrange for
a guided discussion at the meetings of the clubs, on the
subject of the proposed worship exercises.

The meeting of the club opens with the reading of
the minutes which is followed by the treasurer's report,
collection of dues, old business, reports of committees,
reports of representatives of the Junior Synagogue, and
representatives of the Young People's League, new business, good and welfare, in the order named. The regular
club program follows.

It is to be noted that the line of demarcation between
the business and the program is not clearly drawn. This
is due to the fact that much of the program is at grips
with the life of the boy and the club, which is as it
should be. The program should not be an escape from
the world, but a projection into adult life and a contribution toward its enrichment. There are, however,
elements in the program which are purely recreational.
These may follow the parts demanded by the life of the
club. The debates, discussions, readings and recitations
will usually have reference to the immediate objectives
of the club or of the Junior Synagogue. After the regular meeting there follows a social period devoted to indoor games, refreshments, or a session of athletic games
or contests.

The programs of the boys' clubs and the girls' clubs
will differ in accordance with the interests of the mem-
berships of the organizations. It will be found that the
boys' clubs will place more weight on athletics than
girls'—not that girls have no interest in this field. Girls

will be willing to engage in sewing, cooking and baking as an important phase of their programs if there is an attractive worthwhile purpose to be served. Other activities in which girls, as a rule, will be more interested than boys are esthetic and folk dancing, readings and book reviews.

TOPICS FOR DISCUSSION

1. The club consists of twelve boys thirteen to fourteen years of age. There is no adequate talent in the area of music or literature. During the course of the year the Jewish community is interested in campaigns for Religious and Racial Refugees, an inter-religious conference on Tolerance, and a community chest.

Suggest a tentative program or programs for twelve semi-monthly meetings.

CHAPTER X

THE PROGRAM OF THE JUNIOR SYNAGOGUE

The Junior Synagogue includes all the boys and girls organized in the adolescent clubs, and is administered by a council consisting of the president, secretaries, two or more additional representatives of each club, and representatives of the Young People's League. It is desirable that the chairman of the program committee of each club be also a member of the council since it is necessary from time to time to stimulate the thoughts, feelings and interests of the clubs through the elements of their regular programs. The function of the council is to carry forward the objectives of the Junior Synagogue. It organizes itself by electing officers, a president, one or more vice-presidents, secretaries, treasurer, and chairman of a number of standing committees. The duties of the officers are similar to those of other organizations. The function and number of the standing committees will depend upon the size of the Junior Synagogue, its interests and the state of its development. In smaller organizations, several functions are assigned to one committee. In younger organizations without a tradition of standards or interests, the work undertaken will of necessity be simpler, narrower and on a lower plane.

The general aim is to provide activities through which the boys and girls may share increasingly in adult Jewish life. This makes for the acceptance of responsibility for such phases of Jewish activity which are within the limit of their understanding and abilities, and the carrying out of self-chosen tasks in a spirit of sharing with adults the striving and aspiring for which adult institutions and movements have been established.

Present-day Jewish institutions may be divided into a number of categories. There are the institutions expressing and resulting from the sense of relationship between the members of the people. In the international field there is the Joint Distribution Committee for the relief of persecuted Jews abroad; and Hias to facilitate immigration of Jews from hostile to more friendly lands. There are also organizations limiting themselves to special work in these areas, such as the Ort, and the Icor. The number of national and local welfare and philanthropic institutions is legion. Jewish hospitals, orphan asylums, homes for the aged, social welfare and educational agencies dot the land. Some of these organizations are sponsored by members of the Jewish community as a whole—others by large and important fraternal organizations such as the B'nai B'rith, and the Council of Jewish Women, who have also other objectives besides the support of the particular institution.

Another class of organization is devoted to the development of Jewish life in Palestine. The Zionist organization endeavors to foster and strengthen sentiment for the development of a Jewish national homeland. The Jewish Agency of which the Zionist Organization is part, looks to the economic and industrial progress of the land, and raises funds needed for its many undertakings through the annual United Palestine Appeal. Hadassah regards the medical needs of Palestine and certain needs of women and children as particularly within its province. The Jewish National Fund buys land in the name of the Jewish people. The Hebrew University is an institution of higher learning, and also furthers scientific research necessary for the progress of the land and for bringing to light data of historic and archeological value.

The Jewish people are rich in educational institutions. Every community has its religious school. There are also secular Jewish schools which aim to transmit Jewish culture apart from its religious implications. Many communities maintain parochial schools. There are also in many congregations, Jewish high schools. There are also institutions of higher Jewish learning such as the Jewish Theological Seminary, the Hebrew Union College, the Jewish Institute of Religion, the Yeshiva College and the Hebrew Theological College of Chicago; and one may also include Dropsie College which is devoted to Semitic as well as specifically Jewish studies.

Last but not least are the synagogal institutions that occupy a central position in Jewish life and aim to elevate its adherents to ever higher planes of Jewish living. The nature of local synagogues is, of course, well known, and the function of their organizations and institutions are fairly well conceived. In general, they aim to satisfy the religious, social and cultural needs of every age group of the congregational family. The regional synagogal organization also comes within the purview of the Junior Synagogue. Ultimately the value and importance of the national synagogal organizations will become evident.

The boys and girls live also in the non-Jewish world where there are additional institutions and movements making for a happier, healthier and better humanity. It is proper that they come in contact with general civic, social and welfare effort.

The very enumeration of the hundreds of Jewish and non-Jewish institutions and movements poses a major problem. Irrespective of the form of participation and sharing that may be advisable, it is a practical impossibility for the children to undertake even to a slight degree the responsibility for the maintenance of a fraction of the hundreds of worthwhile organizations. On the other hand, the very thought of choosing amongst them is repugnant since it would constitute a denial of the values of those rejected. Then, too, the boys and girls have not as yet any norm or standard by which a reasonable choice may be made. For the most part they do not know of the existence of many of these organizations and are unaware of the needs they are intended to satisfy.

It is important also to consider the forms that their participation might take. The adolescent has reached the stage in which the nature and value of money is becoming clear. He is still supported by his parents, and, accordingly, does not as yet realize how vital money is to his very life and existence, but he is beginning to understand. The giving of monetary gifts has therefore a higher value than in the case of the pre-adolescent. More valuable, however, are the things he can do or make. Time and energy devoted to service are more helpful from a character-building standpoint.

Two additional needs must be met—the association of the institution or movement with the purpose for which it was established must be made clear and immediate to the consciousness of the child. The boy must learn also something about the areas in which these organizations are established, and to develop a sympathetically critical attitude to all of them from the standpoint of the Jewish and human wants they are intended to satisfy.

The following suggestions take into account the above considerations:

I. The Junior Synagogue has a standing committee on cooperation with worthwhile non-synagogal institutions or movements. The committee keeps in touch with the various institutions and movements through the daily and weekly press. It enters into the necessary correspondence and receives literature and reports. The news items, articles, propaganda material form the basis for reports on the work of the different institutions, which are rendered from time to time to the executive council and occasionally to the Junior Synagogue as a whole.

The committee makes recommendations as to activity of the Junior Synagogue with reference to these institutions. Participation may take one or more of the following forms:

1. Correspondence is established with the adolescent clubs and high school classes in Palestine and other lands. The more interesting letters received may be printed in the monthly periodical or read at the Junior Synagogue meetings. From time to time gifts are exchanged. Objects received are displayed at the monthly meetings with cards giving the name of the group sending the gift, as well as the club receiving it.

2. Whenever any of the important local or national organizations conducts a campaign for funds, reports are rendered on the work of the organization, and the Junior Synagogue offers its services. It enlists volunteers to act as ushers and pages at important functions, to help in some of the clerical work, running of errands, and the thousand and one other things necessary to a campaign.

3. At times there are also monetary contributions. They may come either from the treasury, or as a result of a special fund-raising effort on the part of one or more of the clubs or the Junior Congregation as a whole.

4. In some communities adolescents have enlisted in the general civic and humanitarian enterprises. The committee keeps in touch with such movements and arranges for cooperation of the Junior Synagogue with them.

5. The representatives of the Young People's League report on the activities of their society with special reference to those projects in which cooperation is possible.

II. It is important that the boys and girls have an adequate understanding of the value of the institutions and movements towards which they make their contributions. Several measures are suggested for achieving this end.

1. The work of the institutions can be presented by a variety of techniques during one or more programs at the regular monthly meetings. There may be a dramatic sketch involving the work of the institutions. Some groups find it interesting and novel to present a dramatic story as it would be produced over the radio—others like to present it in pantomime. The pageant tech-

nique is also helpful. If there are members of the Junior Synagogue who have evidenced creative skill in these fields, they may be asked to write the material.

It may not be necessary to produce an elaborate number on the program. Orations, reports on the aims and activities of the institutions or movements followed by discussion may be sufficient.

2. Another important medium for the purpose is the monthly publication. Short stories, articles, dramatic sketches, poems, etc., all have their value. News events, the record of achievements, human interest stories are also helpful.

3. Clubs may be asked to devote some time at their meetings to discussions on movements in question. Interclub activities may be useful; debates on related subjects, and club literary subjects. Poems, orations, and short stories may be limited to the fields in which the institutions operate.

4. The worship exercises are very valuable. After the preparatory steps, special prayers may be written and recited. Relevant application of the traditional parts of the prayer book may be pointed out. The sermonette may also treat the problem. This element is important for several reasons: It aids in preparing the children for the sacrifice to be made. It enables the members to see their contribution as something that comes in response to an impulse or feeling of sympathy, not only, but also, what is more important, as an act of *zedakah*, an effort to right conditions which bring so much suffering and misery upon our brothers and sisters. It enables them to see what they are doing in a larger perspective, in relation to the whole problem of bringing

the light of religion to the world, in the hope that mankind may see how folly and shortsightedness bring suffering and unhappiness.

III. The committee presents its plans to the executive council of the Junior Synagogue. After discussion the decisions with reference to the program are communicated to the program committee. This committee consists of the chairmen of the program committees of the clubs, and so has direct knowledge and contact with all the talent available. The recommendations with respect to the activities in the individual clubs are communicated to the presidents of the clubs concerned. The committee on worship is interested in the task of developing adequate and timely worship exercises.

TOPICS FOR DISCUSSION

1. Discuss the problem of duplication and conflict in Jewish life, treating the causes and making suggestions for possible solution.

2. Discuss the advantages and disadvantages of the National Welfare Fund and the National Welfare Council.

3. Discuss the extent to which the adolescent organization may be interested in the above problems. Will the interest be helpful toward a solution? How?

REFERENCES

Cohen, Samuel M. *The Progressive Jewish School*. Pages 36-51.

Karpf, Maurice J. *Jewish Community Organization in the United States*.

CHAPTER XI

THE PROGRAM OF THE JUNIOR SYNAGOGUE
(CONTINUED)

IV. The committee on synagogue activities consists of a number of sub-committees depending on the size of the Junior Synagogue. When the organization is small, the committee will of necessity be small and sub-division will be impractical. When the Junior Synagogue is large, it will be possible for the committee to divide its personnel. We shall present here the functions of the committee which are the same irrespective of the number of its sub-committees.

1. The arrangements for worship exercises. This involves the appointing of leaders for chanting the selection from the Torah and parts of the prayer book. The committee keeps in touch with the clubs or committees on Jewish and non-Jewish institutions. It is informed of the worship needs of the clubs and the events in the outside world to which a worship response would be helpful. It makes arrangements for the writing and reciting of the necessary prayers and chants. If there is a choral group in the Junior Synagogue, it suggests selections suitable for rendition by the group for the exercises. It also develops the inspirational elements of the exercises through arrangements for ever greater

participation on the part of the worshipers, by means of congregational singing and the responsive reading.

In all these activities it is guided by the Rabbi. Even though it is quite proper and often helpful to have one of the boys or girls chant the service and deliver the sermonette or lead in prayer, it should be understood that the intent is not to have the children "play at being a Rabbi." The Rabbi of the congregation is the Rabbi of the Junior Synagogue. It is his responsibility to decide as to the extent to which the members are prepared to lead and conduct the exercises.

V. The Committee cooperates with the school and the congregation in a number of ways.

1. It organizes the traffic regulations so as to insure the safety of the children at nearby crossings during school hours.

2. It arranges for a reception of the school pupils some time during the year, and accepts for the Junior Synagogue a reciprocal invitation.

3. When necessary it arranges for the coaching of the backward pupils of the schools.

4. It arranges for the participation of the Junior Synagogue in the annual Bar Mitzvah and Bas Mitzvah celebration, welcoming the children who have become eligible for membership in the Junior Synagogue, and organizing them into Junior Synagogue clubs.

To accomplish these and other forms of cooperative activity it is desirable that the chairman of the committee represent the Junior Synagogue on the council of the general organization or the students' organization of the school, and that a member of that organization represent the school on the council of the **Junior Synagogue**.

VI. If the congregation conducts a Jewish **High School**, the Junior Synagogue cooperates with it in such ways as the following:

1. It encourages the members to enroll by giving adequate publicity in the monthly periodical to the high school activities, the courses offered, and the notable achievements of the students.

2. It avails itself of the facilities of the school for the training and information necessary for the better accomplishment of the tasks set for its officers, committee members and general constituency. The cantors of the Junior Synagogue, for instance, should be children trained by the school in the meaning of the prayers, Jewish history, etc. Where practical, the principle may be established that certain duties are entrusted preferably to children who have satisfactorily passed certain courses in the school.

VII. The committee arranges also for cooperation with the Young People's League.

1. The members act as pages and messengers at important congregational conferences and meetings.

2. They invite the adults to one function a year and they prepare a program for their entertainment. They also accept an invitation from the Sisterhood and Men's Club for a reciprocal function.

3. They contribute money and useful articles of their own make for the Synagogue and other rooms of the Congregational building or buildings.

4. They participate in the exercises marking the entrance of the school children into the Junior Synagogue, and the entrance of the members of the Junior Synagogue into the Young People's League, at which time the adults also participate.

5. They note major events in the families of their members through appropriate exercises, prayers, visits, etc.

VIII. The program committee consists of the chairmen of the program committees of the various clubs. It arranges the programs for the monthly meetings and festival celebrations of the Junior Synagogue. One of the latter takes place at the regular monthly meetings. Others are set for special times and consist of more elaborate numbers. This committee also arranges for those functions at which other synagogue groups are the invited guests, and for the participation of the Junior Synagogue in the programs to which they are invited as guests. At times the Junior Synagogue may invite a similar organization from another congregation for a social meeting. The program committee prepares appropriate numbers. It keeps in touch with the committees on cooperation, and congregational activities, so that it may help carry out the aims of these committees.

TOPICS FOR DISCUSSION

TENTATIVE CLUB PROGRAM

Boys

Age: 13-14

October, 1936—end of January, 1937

OCTOBER 11

1. Get-together
2. Summer reminiscences
3. Business
   Reports of plans of chairmen of committees on debating, athletics and literary contests
4. Games
5. Athletic Practice

OCTOBER 18

1. Literary and musical meeting
   a. Recitation
   b. Musical selection
   c. Dialogue
   d. Musical selection
   e. Journal
2. Try-outs for debates, literary contests
3. Games
4. Athletic Practice

OCTOBER 23

1. Business Meeting
   a. Financial report—payment of dues

   b. Discussion
      What shall be our contribution to the Junior Congregation program?
2. Games
3. Athletic Practice

NOVEMBER 1

1. Junior Synagogue Program Balfour Day Declaration Program

NOVEMBER 8

1. Business
   a. Report of chairmen of committees
   b. Discussion
      What shall be our Thanksgiving program?
      Shall we cooperate with the non-Jewish clubs?
2. Games
3. Athletic Practice

NOVEMBER 15

1. Reception to Girls' Club
   a. Presentation of entertaining program of musical selections, literary contributions, original essays, community singing, etc.
2. Games
3. Refreshments

NOVEMBER 22

1. Rehearsal for Thanksgiving Day Program
2. Preparation of reception of guests
3. Games
4. Athletic Practice

THURSDAY, NOV. 26,— THANKSGIVING DAY

NOVEMBER 29

1. Business meeting
   a. Financial report, payment of dues, bills, etc.
   b. Discussion
      What shall be our Hanukkah Program?

DECEMBER 6

1. Elimination Contest for debating
2. Elimination Contest for literary contest
3. Journal
4. Games
5. Athletic Practice

DECEMBER 13

1. Hanukkah Program
   a. Welcome to Parents
   b. Musical selection
   c. Recitation
   d. Debate
   e. Contribution to Synagogue
   f. Acceptance of Contribution
   g. Refreshments
   h. Games

DECEMBER 20

1. Visiting Girls' Club

DECEMBER 27

1. Business meeting
   Collection of dues
2. Athletic Contest

JANUARY 3

1. Recitation
2. Original essay
3. Original essay
4. Musical selection
5. Journal
6. Games
7. Athletic Practice

JANUARY 10

Debate with other club

JANUARY 17

1. Discussion
   What shall be our Hamisha Asar Program?
   To what Palestinian institution shall we contribute?
2. Games
3. Athletic Practice

JANUARY 24

1. Business
     Payment of dues, bills
     Discussion
          What shall be our
          Purim Program?
          To what charity shall
          we contribute?
2. Games
3. Athletic contest

JANUARY 27

Hamisha Asar Program
a. Introductory address
b. Palestinian playlet
c. Guest speaker
d. Contribution to Pales-
   tinian institution
e. Palestinian refresh-
   ments and commun-
   ity singing of Pales-
   tinian songs.

1. Criticize the above program from the following standpoints:

   a. Is it sufficiently varied to provide interesting activities for all members of the Club? Explain.

   b. Are the activities suggested adequate for boys between the ages of 13 and 14? Explain.

   c. Is the inclusion of social service activities in the festival celebration advisable? Why?

   d. Is adequate time allowed for the preparation of the program? Explain.

2. Suppose there were a number of members who were interested in arts and crafts. What elements would you introduce into the program so as to permit the expression of these talents for the good of the club, the Junior Synagogue, the synagogue, the home, the community?

3. a. Do you think that the contribution to the congregation made on Hanukkah is an adequate way of expressing the interest of the children in the synagogue work? What other project would you suggest?

b. Are the contributions to Palestine on Hamisha Asar adequate? What other project can you suggest?

c. Can you suggest projects for enriching home life?

d. Which of the projects suggested are suitable for the club and which are suitable for the Junior Synagogue?

4. What elements in the final program suggested the need of help by the leader of the club? What elements need the help of experts?

5. How would you organize the Program Committee? What suggestions would you make as to how it should function? Give an imaginative account of a perfect meeting of such a Committee.

REFERENCES

Sixteenth Yearbook. American Association of School Administrators. Pages 232-257.

McKown, H. C. *Extra-Curricular Activities*. Pages 124-136, 350-443.

CHAPTER XII

THE PROBLEM OF SEX

The most evident difference between adolescence and childhood is with respect to the sexual development and growth. Formerly the general opinion was that adolescence marks the period when the organs of sex and their associated glands begin to grow and develop. The view held at this time is that the development begins with infancy, and that in adolescence the rate of development is notably increased. The maturation of the glandular system at this time also results in the release into the bloodstream of certain hormones that affect the attitudes of the boy or girl to his playmates of the same and opposite sex. There is a greater "mothering" tendency on the part of the girl. It is reasonable to assume that an analogous development in the boy takes on the character of protectiveness, and may be the basis for the phenomena of chivalry.

If there were no complications arising from the pattern of culture in which we live, what would happen would probably be a gradual increase of intimacy between the sexes, accompanied by varied sex play and leading to mating and the founding of families. The complications arising from the interplay of individual tastes and preferences as well as antipathies would not be serious in view of the fact that from the start sexual interest tends to be reciprocal in nature.

Our present civilization, however, results in serious complications and difficulties. First of all, the whole subject of sex is surrounded with an air of mystery and shame. The natural tendency of the indivdual is to refrain from admitting a sexual interest in another until there is some assurance that the interest is returned. This tendency is given a radically different and injurious character by the social acceptance of the conviction that such an interest is immoral, sinful and unclean. The resulting inner conflict often finds resolution in asocial and perverse forms.

The founding of a family necessitates also an economic security and independence which for the majority of our youth does not come until long after they are sexually mature. There is, accordingly, need for postponing the thought of marriage for many years. In a large number of instances, perhaps a majority, there develops an acceptance of the principle that that fact makes permissible sex play of an intimate nature. The boy reasons: "The girl knows I am not in a position to support a wife. She is accordingly willing to join me in a good time for the fun of it." The girl reasons: "Since we cannot marry, why should a girl be compelled to deny herself pleasures which the boy may enjoy? Why a double standard." The conduct and norms prevalent with the older adolescents naturally influence the behavior of their younger brothers and sisters.

Several additional elements serve to increase the difficulties in the situation. The natural desire on the part of the adolescent to establish his independence from the authority of parents, teachers, and other adults ex-

presses itself also in this field. There is added pleasure
in not conforming to the standards urged by parents and
teachers; it is smart to be on your own.

The boy and girl are confronted by a variety of codes
and standards impossible for them to reconcile. In many
homes the subject is taboo. Even where the parents are
modern and do not object to discussing the "facts of
life," the standards as to what the boy and girl may
talk about, or do together, are usually quite rigid. May
they kiss, pet, sing suggestive songs, engage in certain
modern dances? Most parents will confine the sex play
of their children to very formal parties and dances.
The high schools take a position similar to that of these
parents. On the other hand, entirely different standards
obtain in the street groupings or small group sets, and
more private clubs or gangs. The fact that they know
that their older brothers and sisters do not live up to
the stern regulations set up for them does not help any.
Neither does the participation of some parents in night-
club life or wild parties, which, of course, provides rife
material for the untrammeled insights of their growing
sons and daughters.

Much of the leisure time of the adolescents is taken
up by the movie, popular magazine, radio, and stage.
Here he is confronted with norms of conduct, feeling and
thinking, often at variance with those of the parents.
The manner in which the love scenes are presented helps
to isolate for the audience or the reader the physically
pleasurable aspects of these activities, weakening the
more effective safeguards of the moral life. The plays or
stories with a moral do not help much. No matter how
dire the consequences of the transgression, the evil act
is presented with all the glamour necessary for the pro-

vision of a "real kick." The physical stimulation of the
boys and girls is reinforced by the implied general
social approval.

The problems arising out of the sexual development
of the adolescents will not find a complete solution until
there is a radical change in industrial, economic and
political status of society. The biological demands of
the individual cannot be set aside because of techno-
logical and industrial needs. When conflict develops,
society and government have a duty in the direction of
changing the culture so as to prevent the resultant
evils. Although a complete solution is not possible, the
club can contribute its share to the forces making for an
intelligent attitude toward these problems, and for sane
and moral conduct in these fields.

At this point it may be well to attempt to evaluate two
procedures generally acceped as helpful. It is the practice in a number of organizations to have boys and girls
belong to the same club. The reasons advanced for this
are the same as given by those who favor coeducation
in the high school or college. The objectives of the club
are the same for boys and girls. Why increase sex consciousness where it is not essential? It prevents morbid
self-consciousness which may lead so easily to impulsive
misbehavior. Coeducation also provides opportunities
for the little courtesies and niceties which express the
right relationships between the sexes.

Perhaps the strongest argument offered is that cooperative activities with members of the opposite sex
are helpful in building sane attitudes toward them.
Young people must learn to view those of the opposite
sex as persons and not merely as embodiments of sex.

The club situation however differs from that of the

high school and college. In the latter, the boys and
girls actually pursue the same study; in the club, with
its emphasis on individual interests and aptitudes, one
must reckon with the fact that the adolescent boy as a
rule has widely divergent interests from the girl.
Whether there is an innate basis for it, or whether it is
due entirely to the culture in which we live, the adolescent girl will have more to share with other girls of her
age than with boys.

We must reckon, too, with the fact that the strength
of the interest of the sexes in each other sometimes
frightens them. They are ill at ease in each other's company when the occasions for cooperation are too wide
and general. The need of reciprocal approval which does
not always take place, results sometimes in the emergence
of a compensatory pride which expresses itself in a con-
tempt for the opposite sex. Thus the adolescent often
oscillates between extreme interest and equally extreme
diffidence and antipathy toward the opposite sex. This
interferes with cooperative activity, which is the foundation of club life. Experimentation shows that the sexes
do not cooperate very well with each other. The situation is quite different in the average classroom where
each member is on his own, and the activities are paral-
lel rather than cooperative.

Of course, the sexes must learn to cooperate with each
other. The activities of the Junior Synagogue provide
ample opportunity for this. They act together on the
executive committee of the Junior Congregation, where
the standing committees of the central bodies are constituted of boys and girls, and many of the activities
expressing capacities such as dramatics, musicales, etc.,
are conducted by members of both sexes.

Another measure much in vogue these days is the provision of formal instruction in the form of courses and lectures. Subjects treated vary from the physiology of reproduction to the incidence of venereal disease, from the psychology of love to the social implications of marriage. The value of these courses cannot be over-estimated. It is wise to make available to adolescents factual information on the physical process of reproduction. In general, it is a good rule for parents and teachers to respond readily, objectively, and unemotionally to the natural curiosities of boy or girl. This, however, will not materially lessen the frequency with which boys and girls will exchange lurid information and misinformation in their gangs and sets. The motives for such confidences are the same as for reading erotic literature—to enjoy vicariously experiences denied by social and religious precept. In all probability the excited whisperings are no more harmful than the indulgence in Boccaccio or the Arabian Nights.

Nor should it be expected that a knowledge of the very real dangers of infection will serve as a reliable deterrent to illicit intercourse. Fear is helpful, of course, though it is not the best reason for avoiding immorality. The difficulty lies in the fact that the preliminary flirtation and approaches are not regarded as dangerous in themselves. When, as a result of the love play the passions are thoroughly aroused, there is a blocking of the tendency to caution and to prudence. When hunger is strong, even suspect food is desired.

The value of the courses and lectures on subjects like the psychology of life and the social implications of marriage depend on the content of the courses.

More important is the consideration that the springs

of attitude and action are fashioned from innate needs,
habits, and codes developed in the social nexus of the
individual. Formal instruction has its uses especially
when it provides the skills and information which the
individual feels that he requires. The learning must be
preceded and accompanied, though, by a program of
activity through which the proper attitudes are formed.
How will the program of the Junior Synagogue and the
individual club effect this? The following suggestions
may prove helpful:

1. The clubs should be homogeneous with reference to
sex, and as far as possible, with reference to age.

2. The standards of conduct established for the
Junior Synagogue as a whole should make for dignity
on the part of the girl, and chivalry on the part of the
boy. Chivalry, of course, can and has been overdone.
In many cases it smacks of the hypocritical when ex-
aggerated forms of flattery and subservience do not prevent loss of respect and concern for the well-being of the
person. It is anomalous to find men of high gentlemanly
quality in the social sphere utterly neglectful of the
health and sometimes even safety of their female em-
ployees.

There is, however, a value in the natural tendencies
through which the innate differences in attitude of the
sexes to each other find expression. Girls may be es-
corted home after a meeting. It is important, though,
that the boys accompany the girls nearest their homes
rather than those they like.

3. Gossip, the criticism of individuals in their ab-
sence, should be branded as unworthy of the members
of the Junior Synagogue. We help each other overcome
our faults—we do not punish our friends for possess-

ing faults by weakening the respect and friendship they enjoy. This will prevent much of the whispering that often results in dissension and conflict, and which, in the realm of sex, is often motivated by unwholesome and morbid interest.

4. Interest in the opposite sex is seldom purely physical. It often begins when the individual is not even conscious of his physical urges, and does not deepen to any extent without developing concern for the other's well-being, ideals, and future. There is a strong desire to eat together, to play together, and to cooperate for the achievement of shared objectives. Such cooperation, when their purpose is sufficiently personal, can relegate the more physical nature of the attraction. Since the Junior Synagogue was founded for the social and spiritual objectives in life, the boys and girls can find innumerable purposes for which they work together. The reciprocal sexual interest will lend strength and satisfaction to the involvement of their personalities in the ideals they serve. In other words, the fact that they find so much happiness in sharing ideals and working for their realization, constitutes a partial expression of the sexual urge that will rob the physical phase of that impulse of much of its compelling strength. They will be living on a higher plane than the purely physical.

5. The boys and girls in position of leadership in the Junior Synagogue, concerned among other things with the good name of the organization, have available a number of channels through which they could bring to bear upon the individuals, potent social forces that will influence their behavior and their attitudes. All the festivals are associated with the historic and legendary events exemplifying the larger responsibilities and the

greater sacrifices on the part of women in behalf of their people. The periodical, the program of the monthly meeting, the sermonettes of the worship exercises, practically every phase of club activity can be utilized in creating and strengthening the correct attitudes to each other on the part of the boys and girls.

6. Should gossip become prevalent, some original sketches or articles can be used as corrective measures. If necessary, open discussions on the whole subject by the boys and girls can be conducted by their own leaders. These discussions may take place in the individual club or at a conference called by the proper officers, such as the chairman of the program committee.

7. The library should contain books on sex and the problems connected therewith, suitable for adolescents. These should be displayed with all others, and no special procedures should be necessary for their circulation.

To recapitulate. The economic and industrial structure of present-day society prevents a harmonious development and expression of the capacities of the individual. The problem is especially crucial with reference to the sexual growth and development of the boy and girl. While a full solution must await reconstruction of society, the Junior Synagogue can do a great deal to ameliorate or prevent the evils arising from these maladjustments. It can emphasize the special interests of the sexes through the organization of clubs homogeneous with respect to age and sex. It can involve the feelings and strivings of the boys and girls in socialized, spiritual ideals and objectives and can utilize social pressure for developing and stimulating attitudes of dignity and modesty on the part of the girl, and of chivalry and reverence on the part of the boy.

The club started quite auspiciously. There were twelve girls and fourteen boys, about 14 years of age, at the first meeting. Mr. J., the director, took to the children and they to him without any difficulty. After the first six or seven meetings, the children were having such a good time that the word went forth that this was the best club in the building. Only five more children were selected, however, and then the doors were closed.

It is hard to say when the trouble first started. Mr. J. first noticed it at a meeting about a year after the club had been in existence. Mary appeared a little too bitter in opposing a simple and unimportant motion made by Ella. At this time, however, Mr. J. gave it no attention. At subsequent meetings though, the incompatibility between the two girls increased. The dissension spread. Soon the girls were the leaders of two groups. They appeared to delight in fighting each other.

The meetings developed into acrimonious debates that inhibited all action and progress. The members began to stay away. There was nothing the director could do. Reasoning with the girls did not help. Each insisted on her right to express her views for the good of the club. The suggestion that they get together in advance did not avail. "You cannot reason with that girl," was the usual response. "Besides, how do I know what will come up at the Club?"

Two months ago, Mr. J. breathed a sigh of relief. Mary left the club. His joy, however, was shortlived. In two weeks, Ella left also. The rest was a tale too sad to be told.

Thoroughly disappointed, Mr. J. went to see the

Rabbi. "I will never lead another club again," he said. "Two whole years utterly wasted." The Rabbi replied kindly: "I don't think that it is all wasted. The children still have a high regard and love for you. Don't you feel it when they greet you in these halls and on the street?" "Yes," replied Mr. J. "But now that the club is disbanded, these feelings won't last."

A. It is evident that we have here a case where two cliques were formed with the result that the club was destroyed by unnatural growths within it. The fact that the formations began not in connection with any rivalry for office would indicate that the source of the enmity between the two girls lay in another direction, and perhaps was not really known to the girls concerned.

Can you suggest possible reasons for the enmity?

B. Incompatibility between the girls must be ruled out. It would have developed much earlier in the history of the club if it had existed.

Is there a possibility that there was rivalry with respect to some boy in which both might have been interested?

Most of the functions of the club were dances and other social affairs. This might give frequent opportunity for the boys and girls to develop a personal interest in each other. Suppose that were the cause.

Would you say that doing away with dances and social affairs as part of the club program would help?

Would the adoption of such a policy tend to destroy considerable interest in the club?

C. Are adolescents always attracted to the opposite sex?

Are there times when they are repelled? Why?

Do boys and girls work together more efficiently than separately? Why?

In the case of adolescents, is it best to have clubs of different sex, or of the same sex? Why?

If the clubs are going to be of the same sex, is it advisable to create opportunities when these clubs could come together? Why?

D. Would doing away with coeducational clubs solve the problem?

What about emphasis on other objectives than the purely social one?

If there were an emphasis on higher aims and purposes, would that necessarily lead to less intense social activities? Why?

REFERENCES

Anastasi, Anne. *Differential Psychology*. Pages 386-446.

Peattie, Donald C. "A Way to Chastity." *Reader's Digest*. December, 1937. Pages 30-33.

Sadler, William S. *Piloting Modern Youth*. Pages 386-446.

Wieman, Regina Westcott. *The Modern Family and the Church*. Pages 252-254.

CHAPTER XIII

THE YOUTH LEADER

Leaders of youth groups bear a variety of titles; master, leader, guide, adviser, are better known than others. As titles they are not very satisfactory. They do not define adequately the function of the leader, and they often connote a phase of leadership activity that may frustrate the purpose of the club from a character-building standpoint.

The better the leader, the less his method denotes the master. Guide and adviser are better in that the authoritarian element is less evident. On the other hand, there is also absent the one phase that makes leadership effective—that of sharing. Just as is it is important that the objectives of the activities should be desired by the youth—the ends must be those they strive for—so it is necessary that a leader share in the wished-for goals. The term "master" fails to define the youth's participation in the purpose of the activity; the titles "adviser and guide" do not denote that the leader regards the objectives as having values for himself.

The following description represents a meeting typical of a large number of adolescent clubs:

The leader is sitting by the side of the president who turns to inquire,

"Shall we have old business?"

"Yes, certainly," is the reply.

"We will now have old business," to the club.

The discussion and the reports are addressed to the leader as well as to the chairman. The leader interrupts the speakers and expresses his views on every subject considered. As a rule his suggestions are accepted. There is animation and enthusiasm before the meeting and after. During the meeting the discussions of the members are halting and received with half-hearted attention.

It is evident that the members are not vitally concerned with the business of their organization. They go through the motions because it may be pleasant to imitate adults or because they find it necessary in order that they may enjoy the social activities, games, and athletics which come before or after their meetings. The leader obtains his authority on account of his prestige in other fields, such as athletics, or because he may deprive the club of its meeting place and even of its existence.

Leadership of this type may be regarded by many as successful. The meetings are orderly and usually well-conducted. The boys and girls occasionally contribute to adult enterprises. They participate in Flag Day, act as pages at adult functions, and are often ready in an emergency, to respond to direction. Friendships are forged by some of the cooperative activities and may conceivably last a long time.

Unfortunately, few of the members, on attaining adulthood, will affiliate with the welfare, educational, or religious institutions necessary for the advancement of Jewish life. Those that do, respond to home influence and other environmental factors rather than that of the club. The club activities do not result in a broadening and deepening of the knowledge and loyalties of the members.

To the adolescents the club leader is representative of the adult world. His presence indicates a relationship between themselves and adults. In most clubs the relationship is one of reciprocity. The members receive certain privileges; a meeting place, the use of recreational facilities, etc. In turn they abide by rules enunciated by the leader and accept such tasks as may be assigned to them. This situation practically precludes the sharing of objectives.

What is more desirable is a relationship of cooperation. It is important that the boys and girls actually espouse ends and purposes embodied in adult institutions and experience a sense of working together with their elders for shared values.

The difficulty in attaining this end is evident. The distance between them and adult leaders of the synagogue in terms of age and maturity simply cannot be bridged. Even the terms by which the adults identify certain values often imply more than the adolescents can grasp. When together, the boys and girls still feel that they are happier and more at ease when they take orders.

It is quite different with respect to the young people of the Congregation. Youth is not so far removed in feeling and understanding from boyhood and girlhood. Here cooperation is psychologically possible. The machinery for effecting cooperation is also quite simple. The Junior Synagogue is represented on the governing body of the Young People's League. The Young People's

League is represented on the clubs and on the executive council of the Junior Synagogue. Through these reciprocal representations, each body is in contact with the interests, aims, and activities of the other. When the aims are mutually acceptable, there is cooperation, even though each group may exercise a different function, perform a different task, in the achieving of the shared purposes.

The stimuli affecting the boys and girls come from two sources. On the one hand there are the reports to their own body of the representatives of the Junior Synagogue to the Young People's League. They give accounts of the activities and projects of the League that appear important to them. They will naturally emphasize the enterprises in which the Junior Synagogue can cooperate with the League.

The decisions and the plans of the Junior Synagogue naturally affect programs of the individual clubs.

In the second place, the representatives of the Young People's League in the clubs and in the Junior Synagogue report on the reaction of the League to the activities of the Junior Synagogue and its constituent clubs. The approval and disapproval of the League are powerful forces. The Junior Synagogue representatives also convey to the League the reaction of their organization to the activities of the former.

Since the representatives of the League are more mature and possess more ability in the activities constituent to club life, they will naturally be appealed to from time to time for advice and help by the officers and members of the Junior Synagogue. Their tact and understanding will enable them to win the confidence of the boys and girls so that they may even venture occasionally to volunteer advice and help. Under such circumstances they will not be imposing authority; they will be acting as leaders in the democratic connotation of the term.

To remove every possible impediment to free and untramelled cooperation, it is advisable that these representatives should not be known as leaders. The officers of the Junior Synagogue are not called leaders by their fellow members but are denoted by the titles of their respective offices. It is accordingly suggested that they be called representatives or delegates. The effectiveness of their functioning will not be affected by their title or even lack of one.

They sit among the other members of the organization, participate in the discussion as the others do, and exercise a voice and vote in the proceedings. Their reports are rendered under the heading "Reports of Committees and Cooperating Groups."

The representatives of the League should be chosen on the basis of their special fitness for this work. After all, their function is an educational one. They should possess, for one thing, a real interest in their younger brothers and sisters and a love for working with them. As outlined in the first chapter, they should have a thorough understanding of the objectives of the Junior Synagogue and possess the requisite knowledge to enable them to help in the attainment of these objectives. Tact and understanding of the problems of the adolescent are equally desirable.

Strictness, discipline, etc., imposed from without are unnecessary. If used effectively, they may make a good impression on the observer. From the standpoint of character building, however, they may even be harmful.

The aim of the Junior Synagogue in this sphere is in the direction of self-control, self-discipline, rather than the response to authority derived from external sources.

The representatives in the Young People's League should be able to make available the information and materials needed by the clubs in the carrying out of their programs. They should be willing and ready to meet with the groups and committees interested in certain tasks so as to render help and advice. If the projects are of interest to the boys and girls and they are given adequate help in carrying them out, the discipline problem will disappear.

In addition to the official representatives of the League, the Junior Synagogue will also benefit greatly if it can avail itself of instruction and help on the part of specialists and experts in various activities. Athletic coaches, dramatic counsellors, arts and craft instructors, are valuable not only to the individual boys and girls who benefit from their instruction, but also to the club as a whole. The Young People's League endeavors to provide these instructors either from their own ranks or from the community as a whole. Strictly speaking, these instructors and coaches need not share the general objectives of the Junior Synagogue. If they do, however, it will make their work more effective. In the latter case they should be in contact with the representatives of the League as often as it is necessary to avoid possible misunderstandings and conflict.

As pointed out before this, the Hebrew High School can offer courses which will be of help to the boys and girls in their club work. Music, history of Jewish institutions, present-day Jewish life, institutions and movements, translation and interpretation of the prayer book, etc., are courses that can make the activities of the Junior Synagogue more effective. The adolescent organization, in turn, can increase the attendance and strengthen the interest in the Hebrew High School. From this viewpoint the instructors of the Hebrew High School are related to the Junior Synagogue in the same way as the instructors and counsellors of the special activities of the boys and girls. Occasional conferences of the representatives of the Young People's League with these instructors will prove helpful.

The Young People's League, to summarize, should secure from its membership individuals who possess the required interest, knowledge, and skill necessary to act as representatives to the Junior Synagogue. Their principal purpose is to make for cooperative effort for worth-while goals between the Young People's League and the Junior Synagogue. In connection with their activities in this direction, they also help their younger brothers and sisters by trying to obtain for them the instruction they need in carrying out their activities. These representatives constitute the Young People's League committee on the adolescent project. The League in this way assumes a major responsibility in the life of the congregation which gives additional value to its function in congregational life. At the same time this insures a continued flow of new members. The members of the various clubs of the Junior Synagogue will naturally join the Young People's League on arrival at the age when they are eligible for such affiliation.

TOPIC FOR DISCUSSION

1. Discuss the extent to which the adult Congregation is prepared to cooperate in carrying out the

programs suggested. What is its share in enabling the Junior Synagogue to function as outlined? Where may difficulty be expected? What can the Young People's League do? What can the Rabbi do?

CHAPTER XIV

THE JUNIOR SYNAGOGUE AND THE WORLD ABOUT IT

I

The Home

The needs the home can satisfy change with the age of the child. Generally speaking, they evolve from the providing of food, shelter and protection, through the giving of help and assistance to the presentation of objectives, purposes, and ideals through which the social and humanitarian urges find expression. The ties between the child and the parents similarly grow from dependence through teacher-pupil relationships to friendship. The home finds its greatest usefulness in preparing the child for achieving a proper place in the world. It is important accordingly that there exist adequate lines of communication between the home and the world through which the former can exercise its more vital function.

The Junior Synagogue is one of the means through which the adolescent begins to make his way in the world. Its program should not represent a break with the home. On the contrary, the adolescent organization should maintain an interest in it and provide for the expression of the interest of the parents in its own activities, objectives and purposes.

The important events taking place in his home are adequately noted by his club. Serious illness of intimate members of his family, occasions of joy, all events in the home that deeply affect the life of the boy and girl, find a sympathetic answering chord in the hearts of his friends.

Reciprocally, the important steps in his growth in the Junior Synagogue are noted by the parents. They are represented at the welcoming ceremonies of the Junior Synagogue and of the Young People's League.

He shares the festival and Sabbath celebrations in which the parents participate, as guests or hosts. In these various functions the attitudes of the parents and their sons and daughters to each other are characterized by mutual respect and consideration.

More important is the fact that the Junior Synagogue embraces ideals and strives for ends which have value also for the parents. This makes for a community of interests which provide an excellent foundation for the friendship between parents and children that will grow deeper and stronger as the boys and girls grow older.

II

The School

The relation of the Junior Synagogue and the school merits careful consideration. The curricula of religious schools, for the most part, are subject-centered. The completion of the school course seldom if ever coincides with the child's attaining adolescence. Many of the members of the Junior Synagogue accordingly will still be pupils of the school. The possibility of conflict in loyalties is manifest.

Even after graduation there remains a sentimental attachment to the school world. The memories of past events glow more brightly as they recede into the past. Can this feeling be utilized for character building purposes?

Many of the festival celebrations of the school and the Junior Synagogue are planned to include the participation of parents. This creates another source of conflict. Naturally, the parents cannot be expected to attend within the short festival period both a school event and a Junior Synagogue celebration.

The difficulties referred to, in reality, point to an opportunity for increasing the usefulness of the Junior Synagogue. The ties between the children and their older brothers and sisters can be made a means of enrichment to the lives of both groups. Accepting the principle that the relationship between the two societies must be intimate and cooperative, plans may be suggested for activities that will be helpful to both.

The Junior Synagogue undertakes to be helpful in a number of school activities. Among them are (1) tutoring backward pupils, (2) coaching in some of the extra-curricular activities, (3) organizing and supervising the traffic regulations of the children at nearby crossings.

There is reciprocal representation on both bodies providing for inter-stimulation and exchange of information. Through these representatives it is possible also to arrange for joint festival celebrations whenever parents are to be invited.

One of the more valuable results of these cooperative activities is the stimulation of the school children to look forward to the time when they would be Bar Mitzvah or Bas Mitzvah and will become eligible for entrance into the Junior Synagogue. In this respect the relationship between the Junior Synagogue and the school is comparable to that between the Young People's League and the Junior Synagogue.

III

The Congregation and the Sisterhood

The difference in age and maturity between the members of the Junior Synagogue and the leaders of the Congregation and Sisterhood precludes cooperation in any real sense of the term. Even when the boys and girls render service to the Congregation the adults will feel that they are receiving help and the members of the Junior Synagogue that they are responding to requests. Similarly, when the Sisterhood gives a party to the members of the Junior Synagogue or one of its clubs there is no feeling of cooperation. Instead there is gratitude for the treat their parents have given them.

In many congregations the boys who have passed the age of thirteen are organized into a Bar Mitzvah club that has as its principal function the conducting of regular services on Sunday mornings. Members of the Sisterhood serve breakfast at the conclusion of the services.

The following are some of the more important outcomes expected from this project: The boys will gain familiarity with the prayer book. Some of the boys will become proficient in the traditional chants of the daily liturgy. It will habituate the boys to synagoguge attendance. It is a means by which the parents and children cooperate.

It is necessary, however, to note some of the limitations of the value of this project. The expectation that this project will habituate the boys to synagogue attendance will probably remain unrealized. Since the services are not planned to answer their present felt needs in the area of worship, they cannot build up the attitudes that will make for their turning to worship for the strength and wisdom required to rise to higher spiritual and ethical planes of living and action.

There should be a carefully worked out program of worship exercises based on the traditional prayer book and integrated with the deeper interests and higher aspirations of the boys and girls.

The refreshments served and the approval of their elders, implied or expressed, will be encouraging, but their effect will not be permanent so long as the service itself does not answer the felt needs of the Bar Mitzvah boys. There is also the danger that the project might weaken the development of a program for regular worship periods for all the boys and girls of the Junior Synagogue.

It has become customary in many men's clubs to arrange for a father-son's night to which the boys are invited. A dinner is generally arranged for and served by the Sisterhood, and the principal attraction is an address by an outstanding professional or college athlete. As a pleasant and entertaining social evening these affairs are usually successful. Here, too, one must not expect too much in the way of permanent effects on the character of the boys.

The program of the Junior Synagogue offers opportunities for the initiation of cooperative activities between the boys and girls and the congregation. The programs for family night, father-son night and mother-daughter night may be arranged in such a way as to emphasize such activities of the boys and girls that are cooperative in nature. The method is to stress the objectives which these activities serve and to let the representatives of the adolescents and adults speak briefly on the work and congratulate each other on what they are doing.

The help that the adolescents render to the school children can be regarded as an assumption of responsibility towards furthering an important congregational activity. The project is in charge of a committee on cooperation with the Congregation. From time to time the committee may meet with a representative of the Boards of the Congregation and the Sisterhood to discuss its activities. This will reenforce the sense of responsibility and cooperation.

The attitude of the adult representatives can help. Appreciation of what the boys and girls are doing should be expressed in such a way as to indicate that the adolescents are sharing in the purposes of the adults. Occasional expressions of interest in the advice and opinions of the Junior Synagogue committee will strengthen the sense of cooperation.

The annual celebration of those who attain the Bar Mitzvah and Bas Mitzvah during the year can also be utilized for this purpose. Representatives of the Junior Synagogue and the Congregation and Sisterhood participate. The addresses indicate that the initiation of these boys and girls into the Junior Synagogue will make for increased opportunities to cooperate with the adults for the realization of ideals taught in the schools.

IV.

The World Outside the Synagogue

The Junior Synagogue is interested in and establishes relations with institutions, causes and movements that function outside the synagogue. In doing so, it only endeavors to carry out the function of the Synagogue which is to spiritualize and socialize the individuals comprising its fellowship. The activities of the Junior Synagogue will lead the boys and girls to ever greater participation in adult religious, welfare, and educational institutions and causes. This participation will help create, and strengthen ties between themselves and other groups of the synagogue family.

Here, too, the leaders of these various institutions should indicate their sense of cooperation with the Junior Synagogue. The various festival celebrations at which the interest of the boys and girls in other Jewish and non-Jewish institutions find ceremonial expression should often be participated in by adults. This will serve to emphasize the fact that in working and sacrificing for causes making for the increase and enrichment of life the members are progressing toward the realization of the higher ideals of the Synagogue.

TOPIC FOR DISCUSSION

1. Compare with Part two, Chap. 4 *The Progressive Jewish School*. Explain in detail the difference in sug-

gested projects under the various headings and suggested reasons for these differences.

REFERENCE

Cohen, Samuel M. *The Progressive Jewish School*. Pages 158-
164.

CHAPTER XV

THE CONSTITUTION

The constitution of an organization has a number of important functions. It defines the objectives of the association, the shared purposes and ideals which integrate the members of the group. It may go further and set down the qualifications of age, sex, race, creed and character required for eligibility. This is usually done when the members are persuaded that only persons with the described qualities may be able to contribute to the realization of the aims of the group.

In a sense, the constitution is also a blueprint of the skeletal structure of the organization. The various principles of the organizational machine are named and their functions with relation to the whole and to each other are carefully described. Naturally, there will be certain officers and standing committees common to all organizations. Others will depend on the objectives of the particular society.

It will also contain such other procedures, rules and conditions, found by experience to be essential to the efficient and working life of the organization. Many constitutions accordingly contain provisions for the amount of dues, the time of meetings, the rules of order and even the regular order of business.

Adult and young people's organizations find constitutions necessary. There is always danger that the society may turn from its original purpose. There is also the possibility of conflict developing as to the respective rights and privileges of the individuals and groups in the organization. The constitution helps to define and delimit these rights and privileges. In general, the more deeply felt, the convictions and the results of the more vital experience of the organization will find their way into the constitution, so that they may serve to guide the further practices and procedures of the association. When additional experiences or changes in the situation necessitate a different procedure or different principle of action, the constitution will be amended or revised.

One of the things adolescents may profitably learn is the nature and function of a constitution. What may it rightfully comprise to be helpful? When may amendment by necessary? Does it sometimes impede required action? How can the possibility of harm be ameliorated? The life of the Junior Synagogue may provide experiences, helpful in answering these and similar questions. The boys and girls as a rule will want a constitution, if only as a sign that their organization is really adult-like. It is best that they should not be presented with a prepared document, but should be encouraged and helped to write their own. In this way it will be possible to enable them to understand how the constitution will function in the organization and the ways in which the articles and sections can facilitate their activities.

The first article naturally concerns itself with the purpose of the organization. The leader should present questions that will enable the boys to crystallize and put into general terms the purpose of the Junior Synagogue. What will we expect to do through the proposed organization, for the synagogue, the school, the home, the Jewish community, the general community? Do we expect that our activities will help us better to understand Jewish life and ideals, American life and ideals? Can the organization help us to further and to enrich the well-being of Jewish life?

Here a word of caution may be necessary. It is well to resist the tendency to formulate the purpose of the organization in terms of the character of the constituent individual. Character traits are specific in nature. The names "honesty," "integrity," "truthfulness" and so forth have no objective reality, and identify form of conduct widely varying in ethical quality. They accordingly cannot be useful in character training. Then, too, it is wiser to encourage the boys and girls to adopt attitudes that are objective and outgoing rather than subjective and self-examining.

The name of the Junior Synagogue requires but little thought. It is determined by the name of the Congregation. The formula may be either the Junior Synagogue of Congregation —— ——, or the —— —— Junior Synagogue. In the case of the individual club, the name may associate the club with some historic event, name or symbol. Should the boys and girls have no suggestions as to name, the leader may present a number of names with an appropriate explanation as to why the individual or symbol expresses in life or meaning the central purpose of the club. In the case of the names of persons there is the stimulus to imitate the life of the given individual. There should be no effort, however, to make the imitation too life-like. The object is not to form every member in the pattern of Maimonides, BarKochba, or any other great Jewish ancestor. The attention should be directed to the cause and ideal to which the hero was dedicated rather than to the individuality of the hero.

Eligibility for membership will depend on a number of factors. If the Junior Synagogue consists of a number of clubs, the individual enters through affiliation with one of them. If the group is too small to form several clubs, eligibility depends upon acceptance of the purpose of the organization and of satisfaction of the age requirements—thirteen to eighteen in the case of the boy and twelve to seventeen in the case of the girl. Of course, the constitution of each club makes it mandatory that the members be loyal to the ideals of the Junior Synagogue. Affiliation with a particular club necessitates in addition that the prospective member is within the age limit of the members of the club. This article in the case of the individual club will be amended from year to year as the age range of the members changes, or can be worded in such a way as to necessitate no change.

The officers and standing committees are determined by the proposed activities of the Junior Synagogue or the club. Do we need a chairman or president? How is he to function at meetings, between meetings, as the executive? Is a vice-president necessary, a secretary, a treasurer? Are the duties of the secretary too many for one person? How shall they be divided?

What standing committees will be needed depends upon what we think our regular activities will be. If we anticipate the necessity of adding to our membership from time to time, we should provide for a regular membership committee. If not, we should do without one. What about a committee to cooperate with the synagogue, with Jewish communal institutions? Since we expect to have programs at our meetings we ought to provide for a program committee.

Will athletics constitute an important and regular phase of our activities? Do we expect to arrange for competitive games with other clubs? If so, it may be well to include an athletic committee with a chairman or manager to make the necessary arrangements. What specifically shall his duties and powers be? Is the consent of the team necessary for any arrangements he may make? How about the consent of the club? May there be some activities to which only the consent of the team is needed?

Which of the above committees should the individual club provide for in its constitution? Which of the proposed activities can be done through the work of the Junior Synagogue?

What about the financial structure of the club and the Junior Synagogue? For what purposes will money be needed? What should the dues be to the club? Shall the members pay also to the Junior Synagogue treasury or shall part of the receipts of the club go to the Junior Synagogue? How large a part? How shall payment be made? Suppose a member is delinquent? Suppose a club is delinquent? If a club disbands for any reason and there is money or other valuable property left, shall the Junior Synagogue appropriate the same? Why?

The club should be represented on the governing body of the Junior Synagogue. Who shall fix the form of representation? The club or the Junior Synagogue?

Why? To what extent can the representatives bind the club? In general, what are the powers of the governing body over the club? To solve this question, let us think of possible specific circumstances. Can we formulate any principles on the subject?

To cooperate with the Young People's League and to obtain their help in some of the Junior Synagogue activities, it would be advisable that arrangements be made for reciprocal representation on the part of the club and the Young People's League and on the part of the Junior Synagogue and the Young People's League. What shall be the position of these representatives? Shall they have the same rights and powers that the members of the respective organizations possess?

Do we want to cooperate with the school organization? Suggest circumstances. Can we help the school?

Would an arrangement similar to that suggested for the Young People's League be adequate? Shall the club be represented on the school organization or only the Junior Synagogue? Why?

Circumstances may necessitate changes and additions to the constitution. What procedure should be followed with regard to the Junior Synagogue constitution? With regard to the club constitution?

At the first meeting when the Junior Synagogue is organized, a small committee consisting of a representative of each club is appointed for the purpose of drawing up a constitution. The committee attacks the problem in the manner outlined. When the draft is ready, a copy is sent to each club and the representative on the constitutional committee reads it, explaining the reasons for each item. He notes the suggestions for changes or amendments. When the governing body of the Junior Synagogue meets, the proposed constitution is read and on each item the suggestions of the club are noted and discussed. The final decision may be left to the governing body or a majority of the clubs or the members as a whole.

The club constitution is similarly prepared by a small committee, the draft is read and explained at a meeting and then adopted with whatever changes the club may decide.

At the beginning of each year's work one session or part of a session may be devoted to a reading of the constitution and a discussion as to how it worked during the year. Are any sections or articles obsolete? Do developments necessitate additional sections or articles? Is there need for redefinition or amplification? This annual reevaluation will help clarify the conception of the constitution as an instrument defining direction and method.

Before leaving the subject, it may be well to consider another problem in the sphere of organization. This volume contemplates a Junior Synagogue consisting of a number of clubs with each club homogeneous as to age and sex. The optimum number of members in a club would be from fifteen to twenty. This would necessitate a considerable number of adolescents. Many congregations are too small to make possible this form of organization. What can be done? The following suggestions may prove helpful:

1. The principle of homogeneity of sex may be sacrificed to that of homogeneity of age. It is more important that the members of the club be of approximately the same age than that they be of the same sex, the reason being that it is much harder for boys and

girls of divergent ages to work together than for the sexes to work together. If accordingly there are too few adolescents to form a sufficient number of clubs, let the clubs be co-educational and endeavor to keep members of each club within a small age range.

2. When the community is so small as to make more than one club impracticable, adopt a Junior Synagogue program in the club objectives. Standing committees may be provided through which the club as a Junior Synagogue may cooperate with synagogal, non-synagogal institutions, etc.

TOPICS FOR DISCUSSION

1. Procure several constitutions of adolescent clubs and criticize them from the following standpoints:

    a. Are the concepts embodied and language used within the understanding of the adolescent?

    b. Do its articles and sections cover the probable activities and situations the club will experience?

CHAPTER XVI

THE JUNIOR SYNAGOGUE IN ACTION

In order to illustrate the working out of some of the methods and procedures outlined in this volume, this chapter will present several imaginary accounts of meetings and activities of the Junior Synagogue.

I. Meeting of the Committee on Synagogue Activities

Present: A, the Chairman; B, Chairman of the Committee on Cooperation with the School; C, Representative of the Junior Synagogue on the Governing Board of the Young People's League; D, Chairman of the Committee on Cooperation with the Congregation and Sisterhood; E, Secretary of the Committee, F, Representative of the Young People's League to the committee.

A: The meeting will please come to order. E, will you please read the minutes of the last meeting?

The minutes are adopted.

A: I want to report that the ideas we presented at the last meeting were accepted with the exception of the one that we should try to raise $500 to buy a new

141

Menorah for the pulpit. They felt that we could not possibly raise that sum or anything like it. Besides, we ought to help now with the U.P.A. campaign. Their idea is that any direct help for the Synagogue should be given in the early part of the year.

D: I think they are all wrong. There is no special time for helping the Synagogue. Those Menorahs should have been changed long ago and there is no time like the present.

B: Well, there is no use going into this now. Let us time our proposals so that there will be no conflict.

F: I move, Mr. Chairman, that at the beginning of every year we have a joint meeting with the Committee on Cooperation with Other Civic and Communal Organizations so that we can plan our respective activities.

After some discussion the motion is passed.

A: Now B, what can you report?

B: Well, twelve of us are giving two hours a week each in teaching some of the slow school pupils. The rabbi told me that these pupils have made much progress, and that he thinks that they will soon be able to follow the work of the class. I want to report also that J, K, L, M, N, O, and P are taking care of the traffic. Each one gives a day a week and is responsible for the traffic patrol of that day. L tells me that some of his children are too young for this type of activity. Something ought to be done about it.

I suggest that you take it up with the President of the school organization and ask that older children be assigned to the traffic patrol.

B: Thanks. I will do that. There is one thing I want

to report. The school is planning to invite the parents to the Passover entertainment. Our Council ought to know this so that there will be no conflict in date.

A: Right. I will report it. Perhaps, you can arrange a joint entertainment by the school and the Junior Synagogue. Any other reports? New business? The meeting is adjourned.

II. *A Meeting of the Executive Council of the Junior Synagogue*

Present: The presidents and secretaries of the following clubs: Herzl, Maimonides, Menorah, Hadassah, Sosannah, Naomi; Chairmen of the Committees on Cooperation with the Synagogue, Cooperation with Non-Synagogal Institutions, Program Committee, and Athletic Committee; representatives of the Junior Synagogue to the Young People's League and of the Young People's League to the Junior Synagogue; the officers of the Junior Synagogue.

The president calls the meeting to order and after the minutes are read and adopted asks the treasurer to report.

The Treasurer: Receipts since the last meeting were as follows: Dues from the Menorah...$10.25; additional receipts for tickets from our last play and dance ...$25.75; Balance...$60.35, making a total of $96.35. Expenses were as follows: printing...$12.00; postage...$3.26; telephone...$8.30. Here are the slips from the officers and the chairmen of the committees. Total...$23.56, leaving a balance as of April 1st of $72.79. The reason that the balance is so small is because thus far only two clubs have paid their dues: the Menorah and the Hadassah. I would like the representatives of the other clubs to tell us right now the reason for the delay.

The President: Any objections? On hearing none, I will call on the president of the Sosannah first.

President of the Sosannah: Well, our own collections were small. The members don't seem to be paying up, so we thought we would wait.

Treasurer: How is your treasury? Have you a balance? I thought you were quite successful with your cake sale.

President of the Sosannah: Well, we have about $60 in the treasury, but we collected only $5 in dues. So I thought we would wait until we got all of the dues.

Treasurer: That is not fair. We need the money. There is our Lag Ba-Omer party we promised the school. There is no reason why we should be deprived of our funds. If the Sosannah Club has trouble in collecting dues from its members we ought to be told about it and perhaps we could help.

Last year the Hadassah had trouble and we helped them collect about 90 per cent of their dues. We ought not be made to wait just because the Sosannahs failed to elect an active treasurer or secretary.

President of the Sosannahs: All right, don't get sore, we will give you your dues. Our own members will pay up, and our treasurer is okeh. We were just busy with our cake sale.

President: What about the Herzls?

President of the Herzls: We had quite a few unexpected expenses last month. There were flowers for two of our members who were quite ill and then the entertainment of the Sosannah Club will take quite a little money.

Treasurer: That's the best I've heard yet. So you took the money you owed to the Junior Synagogue?

President of the Herzls: What else could we do?

Treasurer: If you want to send flowers and you have no money in the treasury, make a separate collection, and the same thing goes if you want to entertain another club. Don't you think I am right?

President of the Herzls: I don't know. I think the Junior Synagogue and the Herzls are just the same. Didn't we pass last year that the clubs entertain each other? I would like to know what Mr. —— thinks about it.

Representative of the Young People's League: That's a tough question, but I can tell you that all the circles of the Young Peoples' League have their budget and don't exceed it. You know grownups act that way, too. They see to it that the fixed expenses for which they obligate themselves are met first of all. Other expenses are incurred only if they are sure they can pay for them.

President: So you think that the Herzls should pay the Junior Synagogue's dues first?

President of the Herzls: But we just won't have the money, after we pay for the Sosannah party.

President of the Sosannah Club: Well, you can withdraw your invitations.

President of the Herzls:　But we don't want to do that.

President:　What fund raising activities have you had this year?

President of the Herzls:　Well, not much, to tell the truth. Our members have had some pretty tough assignments in high school and Hebrew High School, and we somehow couldn't get down to it.

President:　Do you have to splurge when you entertain the Sosannahs? Couldn't you do something simple and get each member to bring something from home?

President of the Herzls:　You have got something there. I bet it will be fun, too, like a grab bag party. We will send you the dues next week.

The officers of the other clubs promised to send in their dues shortly.

President:　We will now hear the report of the chairman of the Committee on Cooperation with Non-Synagogal organizations.

Chairman of the Committee on Cooperation with Non-Synagogal Organizations:　I have a letter here from Mr. S., Chairman of the U.P.A. Drive that I want to read to you.

Dear Mr. D:

I was very glad to receive your letter offering the cooperation of the Junior Synagogue in the furtherance of the U.P.A. campaign. It is a source of strength as well as happiness to know that our sons

and daughters are ready to take their place by our
sides when we have noble work to do.

You can help in many ways. As in the past year,
you can participate in the flag day with which our
drive will close. On May —— there will be a public
meeting at ——— Hall. We will need five page boys
and ten ushers. Can you secure several volunteers?
We are also presenting a pageant at this time and
we shall need about twenty-five young people for some
of the scenes.

Of course, I shall be very happy if you can make
several suggestions as to what you can do to help.
I am accordingly enclosing an outline of the events
scheduled in the course of our drive.

Yours in the love of Zion,

President: That was a fine letter. I will read it at
the next Junior Synagogue meeting. Let each president get a number of volunteers from his club and report to the chairman. The complete report will come
at the next meeting. Have you any further suggestions?

*Chairman of the Committee on Cooperation with Non-
Synagogal Organizations:* The outline states that on
——— there will be a Palestine rally with a pageant
and motion pictures. Why can't we have a youth rally
for Palestine a week earlier? Let's get all the youth
groups in the city to participate. We can have movies,
a good speaker and charge admission. The proceeds, of
course, will be donated to the campaign.

President: Any comments?

First speaker: It's a good idea but I don't think we

will have time to carry it out. We will have to get together with the leaders of the other groups and that means meetings and conferences.

Second Speaker: Don't forget the postage and stationery.

Third Speaker: Couldn't we get that from the proceeds?

Second Speaker: But we will have to advance it first.

It was moved and carried that the Committee on Co-operation with Non-Synagogal Institutions be empowered to carry out the plan.

President: We will have the report of the Chairman on Athletics.

Chairman on Athletics: We are arranging a basketball tournament with the Junior Synagogue of Congregations A, B, and C. The games will begin the second Sunday in May and will continue every other Sunday through June. I want to say now that Mr. X of the Young People's League has been swell. He is helping us build a fine team and I think we will cop the championship this year.

Report accepted.

President: The chairman of the Committee on Synagogal activities will now report.

Chairman: I have nothing to report excepting that at the beginning of the year we ought to get together with the Committee on Non-Synagogal Activities so that we can plan our program in such a way so as not to interfere with each other.

President: Well, make your arrangements with the chairman of that committee.

The Chairman of the Program Committee will now report.

Chairman of the Program Committee: The next program of the Junior Synagogue is all set. The Hadassah Club is giving the program and while I am not permitted to tell out of school, I can say that you can look forward to many pleasant surprises. One more word, there will also be refreshments, and the Hadassah Trio will play for an hour of dancing to follow.

President: Well, this is a grand way to celebrate their third anniversary. Other clubs will please take notice.

Chairman of the Program Committee: With respect to the May meeting,—

Representative to the Young People's League: Just a moment. Before you go on, there is something that I want to report that might have something to do with the May program.

President: Do you yield the floor?

Chairman : Yes, go ahead.

Representative: At the last meeting of the Young People's League there were two speakers, one from the American Jewish Committee and another from the American Jewish Congress. Each claimed that his organization was the best one to fight anti-Semitism here and abroad. During the discussion there were also mentioned the B'nai Brith, the National Conference of Jews and Christians, and several other organizations. I think we, too, ought to find out what each of these organizations proposes to do and why they cannot get together.

Chairman of the Program Committee: We can arrange a meeting at which representatives of these organizations can give us talks.

First Speaker: More speeches. Good night!

Second Speaker: Just a moment. I want to suggest another plan. How about some of us explaining the work of these organizations?

President: Just what do you mean?

Second Speaker: Well, let one of us explain the work of the American Jewish Congress, another one the American Jewish Committee, and so on.

Representative of the Young People's League: How will that help us understand why they don't get together or how they could get together?

President (to the Representative of the Young People's League to the Junior Synagogue): We ought to find out more about these organizations but we certainly don't want to listen to too many speeches. Can you suggest something?

The representative of the Young People's League suggests that there be a dramatization of the problem in this way: a certain number of members of the Junior Synagogue be asked to each personify the president of one of these organizations; each one should make it his business to learn as much as possible about the organization, its aims, its workings and wherein it differs from the other organization. Then let him imagine that an emergency has arisen and that all these presidents get together for the purpose of discussing what can be done. The principal idea is not to prepare the discussion in advance, but to think out carefully what the emergency should be, then let these participants, thoroughly imbued with the spirit of their parts, endeavor to find the best possible solution.

The suggestion is accepted with the proviso that the representative of the Young People's League act as the chairman for the conference and that he and the Rabbi help in the preparation of the actors for their parts.

Business meeting adjourned and followed by a social half hour.

III. *Meeting of the Sosannah Club a Week Later*

Present: President, Vice President, Secretary, Treasurer, and ten members, and Representative of the Young People's League.

President: The meeting will now come to order. The secretary will please read the minutes.

The minutes are read and adopted.

President: The treasurer will now render the financial report.

The report is accepted.

President: I will now ask the secretary to give a report of the last meeting of the Executive Council of the Junior Synagogue.

Secretary: Shall I give the whole report or each part separately?

First Member: Mr. Chairman, we always have the same question, and we always vote to have the report given part by part. Why waste time? Let Rose give her report seriatim.

Second Member: I would like to know what Miss Levy thinks.

President : Do you want to say something about this, Miss Levy?

Representative of the Young Peoples' League: Why not make one motion that all the reports of the Junior Synagogue be given seriatim?

First Member: I move that the reports of the Junior Synagogue always be given seriatim.

Second Member: Second the motion.

President: Go on, Rose.

Secretary: Well, you know, it is a long name and I don't remember all of it.

President: Go on, Rose.

Secretary: Well, the Chairman of this committee said we got a lovely letter from Mr. S., the Chairman of the U.P.A. You should have heard it at a meeting of the Junior Synagogue.

Third Member: Mr. Chairman, I think we ought to get a copy of the letter, so that we could have it on our files. We also worked.

Fourth Member: I think we ought to get the letter printed in the Review, so all the clubs will have it.

President: Any motions on the subject?

Fourth Member: I move that we suggest to the editors of the Review to print Mr. S.'s letter.

Motion passed.

President: All right, Rose.

Secretary: Secondly, the next meeting of the Junior Synagogue will be swell. The Hadassah has a marvelous program and their trio will play for dancing afterwards.

The May meeting will feature a new kind of dramatic program. The play will be made up and acted right out in front of us. This is what will happen. Suppose a great emergency has arisen, something that is threatening the Jewish people with a great misfortune. Well, the leaders of all the Societies that are trying to help our people will gather to try to decide on what to do. Members of the Junior Synagogue will take the parts of those leaders, and the discussion will be made up right in front of us. Yes, after the meeting the Chairman of the Program Committee told me that one of our members will be chosen to participate in the program.

Fifth Member: It's about time. We haven't had a part in a Junior Synagogue program for months.

Sixth Member: There ought to be a rule that every club be given an equal chance to be on the program.

Seventh Member: I move that the Chairman of our Program Committee report to the Junior Synagogue Program Committee that it is our wish that all clubs be given equal opportunities to take part in the Junior Synagogue programs.

First Member: Second the motion.

President: Any discussion?

Representative of the Young People's League: I think we ought to ask the Chairman of our Program Committee to explain just how the programs are arranged.

Chairman of the Program Committee: It depends mostly on what the activities of the Junior Synagogue happen to be, and what is happening in the other organizations in the city and the country.

For instance, I understand that the program of the May meeting was decided on because our representative to the Young People's League was trying to find out the difference between the various organizations fighting anti-Semitism. We felt that we ought to get some information on the subject and since we don't like speeches, especially when they are dry and boring, we thought of this plan.

Sometimes when we have a campaign on, we arrange a dramatic skit or radio drama that presents the cause we are trying to help. At festival time we put on something in music, drama or pageant that brings out the beauties of the festival. Then, too, if we have a debating tournament or oratorical contest, the finals are run off at the Junior Synagogue meetings.

President: What we want to know is how are the participants chosen? How do you decide as to whether a member of the Sosannah or any other club should have a part in the program?

Chairman: When we need music we look to those who are interested in the musical organizations of the Junior

Synagogue. The Hadassah has a trio. We have a choir for the services, and many members with good voices belong to it. The Menorahs have two good violinists and one fine pianist. We know of it because they participated in the orchestra for our pageant. If we need a good speaker we go to those who are members of the debating teams, or who took part in the oratorical contests. Doesn't that sound logical?

Representative of the Young People's League: Are we represented in any of these activities? Are any of our members in the chorus, for instance?

Chairman of the Program Committee: Well, I cannot say. I have been ribbed very often this year on our lack of Junior Synagogue spirit. They always want to know why our members don't get out for the teams and activities.

President: You have been ribbed! You should have seen what they did to me when it came out that we haven't paid our dues.

Chairman: I think that's the trouble. We don't seem to have the right kind of Junior Synagogue spirit. Why, it is hard to get out the program for our own meetings.

Representative of the Young People's League: You are not such a bad crowd. Look at your cake sale and the fine attendance you get at meetings.

Treasurer: But look at my books. We have collected thus far only $5 and the year is almost over.

Chairman of the Program Committee: And think of the work I put in in getting the girls to volunteer.

President: It looks as though we don't seem to care

much for the Junior Synagogue. We like to meet each other and chat and play games and that's why we come to meetings.

Treasurer: Well, if you like to do so, you should be willing to pay for it. The dues are little enough. Why shouldn't our members pay up?

First member: Well, I know I want to pay, but I forget.

Second Member: So do I.

Third Member: Me, too.

Fourth Member: I forget to save up for the dues. I spend my allowance during the week and by the time I come to the meeting I haven't any money left.

Fifth Member: You took the words out of my mouth.

Sixth Member: I guess that's the trouble with all of us. We don't think about the club and the Junior Synagogue during the week.

Representative to the Young People's League: Was there a time when you did think of the Junior Synagogue and were glad and happy that you were members, when you wanted to work and strive for everything that it stood for?

Fourth Member: When we were first initiated in the Junior Synagogue, I felt as though I was on air. The whole world was different. I was happy to join such a fine group of boys and girls.

Fifth Member: I had a feeling that I was getting into a new world where I could do things.

Ninth Member: It felt fine to have all the men and

women tell us that we were becoming like them and could work together with them.

Tenth Member: The Rabbi was splendid. When he spoke I had tears in my eyes.

Second Member: So did I.

Third Member: Me, too.

Representative of the Young People's League: Do you have any of these feelings now?

Fourth Member: Sometimes, but it goes away so quickly.

Seventh Member: I am glad I am in the Junior Synagogue. I would not belong to any other organization, but I don't get the enthusiasm I had at the time of the initiation.

Representative of the Young People's League: Perhaps what we need is another ceremony so as to recapture for us the spirit of the Junior Synagogue and make us feel more deeply our loyalty to its aims and objectives. If I may, I would suggest that we ask the Rabbi to arrange a worship period at the regular services very soon when we could strengthen our love for our ideals.

Second Member: I think that's a fine idea. It may help other members of the Junior Synagogue.

Third Member: I move that we request the Rabbi to have our service dedicated to our love and loyalty to the Junior Synagogue.

Motion passed.

Fourth Member: I move we pay our full dues to the Junior Synagogue.

Motion passed.

Fifth Member: I move we give the balance of our profits on the cake sale to the U.P.A. and the J.D.C.

Motion passed.

Representative of the Young People's League: Since you are acting this way, we don't need that worship period.

President: I think we ought to have it anyhow.

All expressed their approval.

President: We will now adjourn the business meeting and have our own program.

Program followed by parlor games and refreshments.

IV. Sabbath Afternoon Services
Several Weeks Later

After the scroll is restored to the Ark the Rabbi makes the following announcement.

Rabbi: I have been called on to conduct a special worship period at this time. Joe Goldberg of the Menorah will explain the purpose of the service.

Joe Goldberg: Rabbi and Members of the Junior Synagogue, many of us are beginning to feel that we are sort of letting down on the Junior Synagogue. At the beginning of the year we were inspired by the initiation of the Sosannahs and the Herzls of our organization, and by our fine opening meeting. We kept in mind the high ideals for which we were organized and every one of us gave our time and energy to carry out our program of activities. In the last few months there has been a decided loss of interest. We like each other and we come to our meetings and services. But something has gone out of the spirit with which we carried out our undertakings. There is a lack of enthusiasm which may not be very noticeable now but which threatens the strength of the Junior Synagogue as a whole.

Many of us believe that the reason for it all is the fact that we are losing sight of our great ideals for the Jewish people and for humanity. We have, therefore, asked the Rabbi kindly to prepare a worship period through which we may obtain inspiration and strength for the great work in which we are engaged.

Rabbi: As members of the Junior Synagogue we reaffirm our loyalty to the law of God and His ways.

Let us read responsively.

"Oh, God, we seek Thy help and Thy guidance,
For we know that our powers are feeble and our wisdom
is scant.

Teach us the way in which we should go,
For Thy Torah is a lamp unto our feet
And a light unto our path.
It gives understanding to the simple.

Though our hearts turn to Thee when we assemble in worship,

We too often forget Thee and fail to follow Thy light
In the vain pursuit of selfish pleasures.

> Teach us to know the true secret of happiness
> Which is only to be found in serving Thee and following Thy law.

For Thy law is a tree of life to those that support it
And all that maintain it are made happy.

> Bless Thou our congregation and help us to strengthen it
> By banishing from our midst selfish ambition.

That we may all experience good and know how pleasant it is for
Brethren to dwell together in unity.

Rabbi: We seek righteousness and loving kindness, mercy and justice for us, and for all humanity.

We will now sing Hymn:————.

Rabbi: Let us read responsively: The Call to Righteousness.

"Open thy mouth for the helpless,
In the cause of all such as are appointed to destruction.

Open thy mouth, judge righteously,
And plead the cause of the poor and needy.

Whoso stoppeth his ears at the cry of the poor,
He also shall cry himself, but shall not be answered.

He that oppresseth the poor blasphemeth his Maker;
But he that is gracious unto the needy honoureth him.

The merciful man doeth good to his own soul;
But he that is cruel troubleth his own flesh.

When the righteous are increased, the people rejoice;
But when the wicked heareth rule, the people sigh.

By the blessing of the upright a city is exalted;
But it is overthrown by the mouth of the wicked.

Righteousness exalted a nation;
But sin is a reproach to any people.

Where there is no vision, the people cast off restraint;
But he that keepeth the law, happy is he.

Better is a little with righteousness,
Than great revenues with injustice.

Better is little with the fear of the Lord,
Than great treasure and turmoil therewith.

Better is a dinner of herbs where love is,
Than a stalled ox and hatred therewith.

The righteousness of the sincere shall make straight
  his way;
But the wicked shall fall by his own wickedness.

Lord, I love the habitation of Thy house,
And the place where Thy glory dwelleth.

My soul yearneth, yea, even pineth for the courts of
the Lord;
My heart and my flesh sing for joy unto the living God.

In the abundance of Thy loving kindness will I come
into Thy house;
I will bow down toward Thy holy temple in worshipping
Thee.

Happy is the man whom Thou choosest, and bringest
near,
That he may dwell in Thy courts;

May we be satisfied with the goodness of Thy house,
The holy place of Thy temple.

Lord, who shall sojourn in Thy tabernacle?
Who shall dwell upon Thy holy mountain?

He that walketh uprightly, and worketh righteousness,
And speaketh truth in his heart;

That hath no slander upon his tongue,
Nor doeth evil to his fellow,
Nor taketh up a reproach against his neighbor.

Who shall ascend unto the mountain of the Lord?
And who shall stand in His holy place?

He that hath clean hands, and a pure heart;
Who hath not taken My name in vain,
And hath not sworn deceitfully.

He that worketh deceit shall not dwell within My house;
He that speaketh falsehood shall not be established
before Mine eyes.

Mine eyes are upon the faithful of the land, that they
may dwell with Me;
He that walketh in a way of integrity, he shall minister
unto Me.

The Lord is nigh unto all them that call upon Him.
To all that call upon Him in truth.

So have I looked for Thee in the sanctuary,
To see Thy power and Thy glory.

For Thy loving-kindness is better than life;
My lips shall praise Thee."

We will now sing: —————.

Sermonette by Rabbi "How the Junior Synagogue
creates and strengthens friendship."

The service is concluded with the Amidah, Olenu,
Kaddish, etc. The closing prayers refer to the sermon.

TOPICS FOR DISCUSSION

1. What principles treated in this book are illus-treated in this chapter?

2. Would boys and girls talk and act as they are depicted in this chapter?

3. Discuss the way in which the representatives of the Young People's League function, resolving difficult situations and carrying forward the work of the Junior Synagogue.

4. Discuss the ways in which the progress of and life of the Junior Synagogue is interrelated with the world about it.

CHAPTER XVII

TOOLS

The leader as well as the members of the Junior Synagogue will require books, periodicals, manuals and helps of various kinds. It is advisable to begin to build a special library devoted to the needs of the adolescents and the leaders.

This chapter will make a number of suggestions as to the contents of the library. It should be remembered too, that many of the national adolescent organizations are continually publishing newer and better material and that psychologists, sociologists and other scientists are publishing from time to time the results of their experiments and investigations, which may prove of value to the leader. It would be advisable then that from time to time the leaders consult the bibliographies so that their libraries may be abreast with progress in the related fields.

The addresses of publishers and organizations listed here may change from time to time. It is accordingly advisable that current year books be consulted. For Jewish organizations, consult the American Jewish Year Book published annually by the Jewish Publication Society, Philadelphia, Pa. This contains a list of all national organizations and their addresses. The Yearbook of American Churches, published by the Federal Council of the Churches of Christ, contains the names and addresses of Christian national religious bodies. The Education Index contains a list of the names and addresses of the publishers of educational books and periodicals.

I. DIRECTORIES OF ORGANIZATIONS

There are several good directories of adolescent organizations. Especially recommended are:

Pendry, Elizabeth R. and Hartshorne, Hugh. *Organizations for Youth.* McGraw-Hill Book Company, Inc. New York and London. 1935.

Lindsay, Mary R. and Rauchmans, Alexander. *Directory of Youth Organizations.* National Youth Administration of New York City, 264 West 14 Street, New York, N. Y. Ten cents.

Chambers' Youth Serving Organizations. American Council on Education. Washington, D. C. 1937. 327 pp.

Directory of Youth Organizations. 105 pp. mimeo. The Experiment in International Living, Inc. Putney, Vt.

A compilation of organizations all over the world doing work with the youth. Includes important data on programs and achievements.

II. SOURCE ORGANIZATIONS

A number of organizations, commercial and otherwise, publish from time to time material that will be of help to the club and the club leader. It is well to know these organizations and be in touch with them. Many of their publications can be of direct help in building the Junior Synagogue program and others can be utilized with some small modifications. Among these organizations the following may be listed:

The Jewish Welfare Board, 71 West 47th Street, New York, N. Y.

All types of material, including music, games, leaders' guides, etc.

The Department of Synagogue and School Extension, Union of American Hebrew Congregations, Merchants Building, Cincinnati, Ohio.

"The Youth Leader" and other helpful program material.

The Chicago Board of Jewish Education, 30 North Dearborn Street, Chicago, Ill.

The United Synagogue of America, 3080 Broadway, New York, N. Y.

A. Z. A., 1003 K Street, N. W., Washington, D. C.

The Junior Hadassah, 1860 Broadway, New York, N. Y.

Habonim, 275 Seventh Avenue, New York, N. Y.

Hashomer Hatzair, 305 Broadway, New York, N. Y.

Histadruth Hanoar Haivri, 111 Fifth Avenue, New York, N. Y.

National Council of Jewish Juniors, 625 Madison Avenue, New York, N. Y.

Young Judaea, 111 Fifth Avenue, New York, N. Y.

Order Sons of Zion Youth Council, 303 Fourth Ave., New York, N. Y.

Avukah, 111 Fifth Avenue, New York, N. Y.

Metropolitan Leaders Association of the Jewish Welfare Board, 220 Fifth Avenue, New York, N. Y.

The Furrow Press, 150 Eastern Parkway, Brooklyn, N. Y.

It is well to keep in touch with the publications of the following non-Jewish organizations:

The Boy Scouts of America, 2 Park Avenue, New York, N. Y.

Girl Scouts, Inc., 570 Lexington Avenue, New York, N. Y.

Camp Fire Girls, Inc., 41 Union Square, New York, N. Y.

The Boys' Club of America, Inc., 381 Fourth Avenue, New York, N. Y.

Junior Achievement, Inc., 33 Pearl Street, Springfield, Mass.

Junior Red Cross, Washington, D. C.

The Girls Friendly Society, 386 Fourth Avenue, New York, N. Y.

Director of Young People's Work, International Council of Religious Education, 203 North Wabash Avenue, Chicago, Ill.

The Christian Quest. (Publ.)

The state organizations as well as the national organizations of the 4H clubs publish helpful material from time to time. While emphasis in this organization is on the rural population and interests, a great deal of the material provided will be of help also to those in urban communities.

Edith J. Webb. *Boys and Girls 4H Clubs in the United States*. Washington. U. S. Department of Agriculture. Extension Service. Office of Cooperative Extension Work. 1932. 217 pages, mimeographed.

Contains a list of references published since 1910 dealing with all phases of 4H club work.

Youth Builders, Inc., 220 Fifth Avenue, New York, N. Y. Issues a monthly journal, the Young Builders Log and Weekly Bulletin under the title: "Lets Face It Together."

Contains bibliographies, plays, games, etc.

Educational Radio Script Exchange of the Federal Education Committee, Education Office of the Department of the Interior, Washington, D. C., provides radio scripts dealing with historic, literary subjects and problems, current events. The Exchange has also issued a handbook on sound effects which would be helpful in arranging for imitation radio programs which are sometimes quite effective.

The Foreign Policy Association, 8 West 40th Street, New York, N. Y., issues handbooks on various present-day problems in the field of economics, civics, international relationships which are quite helpful for reference.

The Public Affairs Committee, 8 West 40th Street, New York City.

Saves pamphlets on important national and international subjects.

III. BIBLIOGRAPHIES

The best and most complete as well as the latest contributions in related fields are listed in the "Education Index". From time to time this Index should be consulted under the headings "Adolescence", "Secondary Education", "Extracurricular Activities", etc.

The more important youth organizations publish valuable material which the "Education Index" lists under the headings of the specific organization, such as the Boy Scouts, the Girl Scouts, etc. The Index can be consulted at most university libraries and in the larger libraries.

The Index also lists publications of the U. S. Office of Education, and of the National Education Association.

The American Youth Commission of the American Council on Education, Washington, D. C., publishes monthly bulletins containing lists of annotated articles and books classified under such headings as "Vocational Guidance", "Leadership", "Negro Education", and "Delinquency", etc.

In 1938 the Council published a bibliography under the name of "American Youth" by Menefee and Chambers, which contains thousands of annotated articles and books adequately classified.

Jesse L. Murrel. The Program Supplement, Board of Education of the Methodist Episcopal Church, Chicago, 740 Rush Street. 1938. Fifteen cents.

655 titles of pamphlets classified into 12 areas of human experience, such as, citizenship, economics, friendship, personal religious experience, world relationship,—booklets listed suitable for use in conferences and discussion groups.

Benson Y. Landis has compiled an excellent bibliography on democracy. It is published by the Association Press, 347 Madison Avenue, New York, N. Y. Ten cents.

The Metropolitan Leaders Association of the Jewish Welfare Board, 220 Fifth Avenue, New York, N. Y., has a helpful bibliography in their mimeographed publication "Aids to Club Leaders". Fifty cents.

The Society for the Advancement of Judaism, 15 West 86th Street, New York, N. Y., publishes a bibliography in their "Annual Diary" which appears revised and amplified in September of each year. This bibliography is classified under the headings of "History", "Bible", "Jewish Philosophy", "Philosophy", "Philosophy of Judaism", "Jewish Literature", "Collections and Anthologies", "Zionism", "Palestine", "Jewish Religion", "Essays", "Biography", "Fiction and Drama", "Religion and Philosophy", "Jewish Music", and "Hebrew".

The catalogs of the following organizations should be consulted from time to time:

The Jewish Publication Society. Philadelphia, Pa.

The Bloch Publishing Company, 31 West 31st Street, New York, N. Y.

Behrman's Jewish Book House, 1261 Broadway, New York, N. Y.

IV. BOOKS FOR THE LIBRARY

BOOKS REFERRED TO IN BODY OF THIS VOLUME

American Association of School Administrators. *Sixteenth Yearbook*. Washington, D. C. 1938.

Anastasi, Anne. *Differential Psychology*. Macmillan Company. New York. 1937.

Averill, L. A. *Adolescence: A Study in the Teen Years*. Houghton, Mifflin Co. Boston. 1936.

Brooks, Fowler D. *The Psychology of Adolescence*. Houghton, Mifflin Co. Boston. 1929.

Cohen, Samuel M. *The Progressive Jewish School*. United Synagogue of America. N. Y. 1932.

Dimock, Hedley S. *Rediscovering the Adolescent*. Association Press. New York. 1937.

Eisenstein, Ira. *What We Mean By Religion*. Behrman's Jewish Book House. New York. 1938.

Greenstone, J. H. *The Jewish Religion*. Jewish Chautauqua Society, Philadelphia. 1920.

Groves, Ernest M. *Personality and Social Adjustment*. Longmans, Green & Co. New York. 1931.

Hollingworth, Leta S. *The Psychology of the Adolescent*. D. Appleton-Century Co., Inc. N. Y. 1928.

Jersild, Arthur T. *Child Psychology*. Prentice-Hall, Inc. N. Y. 1933.

Karpf, Morris J. *Jewish Community Organizations in the United States*. Bloch Publishing Company. New York. 1938.

McKown, H. C. *Extra-Curricular Activities*. The Macmillan Company. New York. 1937.

Peattie, Donald C. *A Way to Chastity*. Readers' Digest. December. 1937.

Sadler, William S. *Piloting Modern Youth.* Funk and Wagnalls Company. New York. 1934.

Schauss, Hayyim. *The Jewish Festivals.* Union of American Hebrew Congregations. Cincinnati. 1938.

Singer Prayer Book. Bloch Publishing Co. New York, N. Y.

Young, Paul Thomas. *Motivation of Behavior.* J. Wiley & Sons, Inc. N. Y. 1936.

Wieman, Regina Westcott. *The Modern Family and the Church.* Harper & Brothers. N. Y. 1937.

Zubin, Joseph. *Choosing A Life Work.* Union of American Hebrew Congregation. Cincinnati. 1937.

PSYCHOLOGY OF THE ADOLESCENT

For a better understanding of the psychology of the adolescent from the standpoint of the club leader, the following books will be helpful:

Averill, Lawrence A. *Adolescence: A Study in the Teen Years.* Houghton, Mifflin Co. Boston. 1936.

Dimock, Hedley S. *Rediscovering the Adolescent.* Asssociation Press. New York.

Nagle, Urban. *A Empirical Study of the Development of Religious Thinking in Boys from Twelve to Sixteen Years Old.* Catholic University of America. Washington. 1934.

PERSONALITY PROBLEMS

The following six books are valuable for an understanding of the personality of the adolescent and his development and problems:

Burnham, William H. *The Wholesome Personality: A Contribution to Mental Hygiene.* D. Appleton-Century Company. New York. 1932.

Elliott, Grace Loucks. *Understanding the Adolescent Girl.* Henry Holt and Co. New York. 1930.

Heaton, Kenneth L. *Character Building Through Recreation.* University of Chicago Press. Chicago. 1929.

Hopkins, L. T. and others. *Integration: It's Meaning and Application.* D. Appleton Century Co. New York.

Sayles, Mary B. *The Problem Child at Home.* Commonwealth Fund. New York. 1932. (first printing 1928).

Sayles, Mary B. and Mudd, Howard W. *The Problem Child in School.* Commonwealth Fund. New York. 1929. (first printing 1925)

Wallen, J. E. W. *Personality Maladjustments and Mental Hygiene.* McGraw-Hill. New York. 1935.

LEADERSHIP

Arnold, Frances P. *Leaders of Young People.* The Girls Friendly Society. New York. Fifty cents. 1937.

Bogardus, E. S. *Leaders and Leadership.* Appleton-Century Co. New York. 1934.

Busch, H. M. *Leadership in Group Work.* Association Press. New York. 1934.

Ledlie, John A. *Problem Situations in Hi-Y Groups.* Association Press. New York. Twenty-five cents. 1938.

National Association for Study of Group Work. *Exploring Group Work.* Association Press. New York. Fifty cents. 1936.

Partridge, Ernest De Alton. *Leadership Among Adolescent Boys.* Contribution to Education No. 608, Teachers College, Columbia University. New York. 1934.

Pigors, P. J. W. *Leadership or Domination.* Houghton-Mifflin Co. Boston. 1935.

Tead, O. *The Art of Leadership.* McGraw-Hill Book Company. 1935.

SOCIAL PROCESSES

Coyle, Grace L. *Social Process in Organized Groups.* Richard R. Smith. New York. 1930.

Coyle, Grace L. *Studies in Group Behavior.* Harper & Bros. New York. 1937.

Eliott, H. S. *Process of Group Thinking.* Association Press. New York. 1928.

Slawson, S. R. *Creative Group Education.* Association Press. New York. 1937.

VOCATIONAL GUIDANCE

Occupational Index. 551 Fifth Ave., New York. A continuous bibliography of current pamphlets, books, and magazine articles which contain occupational information that will be helpful to an individual in choosing a field of work. Each reference is annotated, and indexed by occupation. Covers all new books; all U. S. Government publications; pamphlet publications of 500 research bureaus, professional and trade associations, educational institutions, etc.; and 100 technical and general magazines. Prepared by National Occupational Conference under a grant from Carnegie Corporation of New York.

B'nai Brith, 1003 K St. N. W. Washington, D. C., has established a department on vocational guidance which is making surveys and issuing pamphlets on various phases of the subject.

Kitson, Harry D., and Crane, M. *Measuring Results of Vocational Guidance: A Summary of Attempts, Occupations,* 16:837-42, June 1938. Booklet. (A bibliography and summary).

Nall, T. Otto. *New Occupations for Youth.* Association Press. New York. 1938.

National Youth Administration of Illinois, William J. Campbell, State Director, Merchandise Mart, Chicago, Ill., has published a series of 29 research reports on different vocations. Booklets. A limited number of these reports are available free. They cover a number of occupations and vocations.

Sobel, Louis H. and Sanler, Joseph. *Group Methods in Vocational Guidance.* The Furrow Press. New York. 1938. Seventy-five cents. Lower rates in quantities.

Strathmore, Ralph. *Planning a Career Through Vocational Guidance*. Strathmore Guidance Bureau. New York. 1935.

White, J. Gustav. *Finding Your Work*. Association Press. New York. 1938.

Zubin, Joseph. *Choosing A Life Work*. Union of American Hebrew Congregations. Cincinnati. 1937.

SEX PROBLEMS

The American Social Hygiene Association, 50 West 50th Street, New York, N. Y. and the Association Press, 347 Madison Avenue, New York, N. Y., publish important books, pamphlets, and tracts from time to time.

The following books and articles are suggested:

Clarke, Edwin Leavett. *Petting—Wise or Otherwise*. Asssociation Press. New York. 1939. Twenty-five cents.

Corner, George W., M. D. *Attaining Manhood*. Harper and Bros. New York. 1938.

Elliott, Grace L. and Bone, Harry. *The Sex Life of Youth*. Association Press. New York. 1929.

Newcomb, Theodore. "Recent Changes in Attitudes Toward Sex and Marriage." *American Sociological Review*. 2:659-67, Oct. 1937.

U. S. Public Health Service. *Healthy, Happy Womanhood: A Pamphlet for Adolescent Girls and Young Women*. V. D. Bulletin No. 60. Washington: Government Printing Office. 1934.

U. S. Public Health Service. *Keeping Fit: A Pamphlet for Adolescent Boys*. V. D. Pamphlet No. 53. Washington: Government Printing Office. 1934.

PROPAGANDA

It is becoming increasingly more evident that something must be done to educate our boys and girls as to the methods and dangers of propaganda. It would be well if the leader did some reading in this field so that he could personally realize the tremendous power of propaganda and the pitfalls that it digs for the feet of the unwary sojourner in life. The following are valuable:

Doob, Leonard W. *Propaganda: Its Psychology and Technique.* Henry Holt & Co. New York. 1935.

Ellis, Elmer (editor). *The Seventh Yearbook of the National Council for Social Studies.* Lawrence Haall, Harvard University, Cambridge, Mass. 1937 Devoted to education against propaganda.

Institute of Propaganda Analysis. *Propaganda: How to Recognize and Deal With It.* New York. 1938. Contains a very good bibliography on the subject.

GAMES, ATHLETICS, ETC.

Games, athletics, stunts will constitute major elements of the programs of adolescent clubs. There are a number of organizations that are continually publishing newer and better material in this area. Of the greatest importance are the publications of the National Recreation Association, 315 Fourth Avenue, New York, N. Y. It is well to keep in touch with their publications.

The following books are valuable:

American Sports Publishing Company. *The Athletic Handbook.* New York. 1936. Twenty-five cents.

Bancroft, Jessie Hubbell. *Games.* Macmillan Co. New York. 1937.

Hughes, William L. *The Book of Major Sports.* A. S. Barnes & Co. New York. 1938.

Mason, Bernard S. and Mitchell, Elmer D. *Active Games and Contests.* A. S. Barnes & Co. New York. 1935.

McCormick, Olive. *Water Pageants, Games and Stunts.* A. S. Barnes & Company. New York. 1933.

National Recreation Association. *Handbook for Recreation Leaders.* New York. 1936. Thirty cents.

Jacobs, Helen H. *Modern Tennis*. The Bobbs-Merrill Company. Indianapolis. 1933.

Post, Julia H. and Shirley, Mabel J. *Selected Recreational Sports for Girls and Women*. A. S. Barnes & Company. New York. 1933.

Ranck, Wilson M. (compiler). "Guide to Sports and Outdoor Recreations; A Selected List of Books, 1918 to December 31, 1934." *The Research Quarterly of the American Physical Education Association*. Vol. VI. p. 149-151. Ann Arbor, Mich.

Rohrbough, Lynn. *Handy 1, Handy 2, Handy 3*.

Staff of the Intramural Sports Dept. *Sports for Recreation and How to Play Them*. (University of Michigan.) A. S. Barnes & Company. New York. 1936.

DANCING

Young Judaea, 111 Fifth Avenue, New York, N. Y. publishes a number of dances for various holidays.

The following books are suggested:

Ballwebber, Edith. *Group Instruction in Social Dancing*. A. S. Barnes & Company. New York. 1938.

Burchenal, Elizabeth. *Folk-Dances from Old Homelands*. G. Schirmer. New York. 1922.

Frost, Helen. *Tap, Caper and Clog*. (Fifteen character dances.) A. S. Barnes & Company. New York. 1931.

Hillas, Marjorie. *Tap Dancing*. (14 routines with descriptions and references to appropriate music.) A. S. Barnes & Company. New York. 1931.

Hinman, Mary Wood. *Gymnastics and Folk Dancing*. A. S. Barnes & Company. New York. 1930.

Joiner, Betty. *Costumes for the Dance*. A. S. Barnes & Company. New York. 1937.

Marsh, Agnes and Marsh, Lucille. *The Textbook of Social Dancing.* Fischer. 1934.

Ryan, Grace L. *Dances of Our Pioneers.* A. S. Barnes & Company. New York. 1928.

Shambaugh, Mary E. *Folk Dances for Boys and Girls.* A. S. Barnes & Company. New York. 1929.

DRAMA

The following are the more important sources for plays:

Samuel French & Co., 25 W. 45th Street, New York, N. Y. Catalogs of annotated plays.

Walter H. Baker Co., 178 Tremont Street, Boston, Mass. Special booklets listing annotated Jewish plays.

The W. P. A. Federal Theatre Project of New York, 303 West 42nd Street, New York, N. Y. Mimeographed list of non-royalty plays and one-act plays. October, 1936.

The National Play Bureau, Federal Theatre Project, 303 West 42nd Street, New York, N. Y. List of Jewish non-royalty plays and projects, historical and general, annotated. Twenty-five cents. List of patriotic holiday plays, dealing with American historic characters and festivals, including pageants, dramas, fantasies, etc. 1937. Twenty-five cents. *Anti-War Plays* is also very useful. Twenty-five cents.

The National Conference of Christians and Jews. Pageants and playlets available from the Chicago office, 203 Wabash, Chicago, Ill.

The Young People's League of the United Synagogue of America, 3080 Broadway, New York, N. Y. List of plays, annotated, suitable for the older boys and girls.

The Jewish Welfare Board, 71 West 47th Street, New York, N. Y., occasionally runs dramatic contests, the prize winning plays often being very good.

The dramatic contest run annually by Temple Israel of Boston, Mass., has resulted in the creation of a number of very fine plays. It is well to keep in touch with them. These plays may be secured in typewritten or mimeographed form. Others have been printed and published.

Furrow Press, 150 Eastern Parkway, Brooklyn, N. Y.

PLAY PRODUCTION

The following books are suggested:

Andrews, Lee and Bruce Weirick. *Acting and Play Production.* Longmans, Green & Co. New York. 1925.

Bricker, Herschel L. *Our Theater Today.* Samuel French. New York. 1936.

Brown, Gilmour and Garwood, Alice. *General Principles of Plya Direction.* Little, Brown and Co. Boston. 1935.

Clark, Barrett H. *How to Produce Amateur Plays.* Little Brown & Co. Boston. 1935.

Hobbs, Mabel. *Play Production (a guide for the inexperienced play producer).* National Recreation Association. New York. 1933. Fifty cents.

Koch, Frederick Henry and others. *Play Producing for School and Little Theatre Stages.* The University of North Carolina Press. (University of North Carolina Ext. Bulletin, v. 15, no. 1). Chapel Hill, N. C. 1935.

Latham, Jean Lee. *555 Pointers for Beginner Actors: do's and don'ts of drama.* The Dramatic Pub. Co. Chicago. 1935.

Smith, Milton. *The Book of Play Production.* D. Appleton-Century Co., Inc. New York. 1935.

STAGE LIGHTING

The following books are adequate:

Bricker, Herschel L. *Our Theatre Today.* Samuel French, New York.

Lighting the Stage with Home-Made Equipment. Baker's Plays. Boston. 1933.

Nelms, Henning. *Lighting the Amateur Stage; a practical layout.* Theatre Arts, Inc. New York. 1931.

Selden, Samuel and Sellmann, H. D. *Stage Scenery and Lighting; a handbook for non-professionals.* F. S. Crofts & Co. New York. 1936.

Wilson, Angus. *Home-made Lighting Apparatus for the Amateur Stage.* H. F. W. Deane & Sons. London. 1936.

COSTUMING

Barton, Lucy. *Historic Costume for the Stage.* Baker's Plays. Boston. 1935.

Grimball, Elizabeth B. and Wells, Rhea. *Costuming a Play.* The Century Company. New York. 1935.

Haire, Frances H. *The Folk Costume Book.* A. S. Barnes Company. New York. 1927.

Norris, Herbert. *Costume and Fashion.* Volumes 1 & 2. J. M. Dent & Sons, Ltd. London. E. P. Dutton & Co. New York. 1924-27.

Sage, Elizabeth. *A Study of Costume.* Charles Scribner's Sons. New York. 1926. Contains illustrations of how historic costumes may be made from modern patterns.

Saunders, Dorothy L. *Costuming the Amateur Show.* Samuel French. New York. 1937.

Truman, Nevil. *Historic Costuming.* Pitman Publishing Corp. Inc. 1937.

Walkup, Mrs. F. *Dressing the Part.* F. S. Crofts. New York. 1938.

MAKE-UP

Baird, John K. *Make-Up*. Samuel French. New York. 1930.

Chalmers, Helena. *The Art of Make-Up*. D. Appleton-Century Company. New York. 1925.

Strenkovsky, Serge. *The Art of Make-Up*. E. P. Dutton Company. New York. 1937.

ACTING

Alberti, Madame Eva. *A Handbook of Acting*. Samuel French. New York. 1932.

Boleslavski, Richard. *Acting; the first six lessons*. Theatre Arts, Inc. 1933.

Calvert, Louis. *Problems of the Actor*. Henry Holt. New York. 1918.

Cartmell, Van H. *A Handbook for the Amateur Actor*. Samuel French. New York. 1937.

Chalmers, Helena. *Modern Acting*. D. Appleton-Century & Co. New York. 1930.

Mackay, Edward and Alice. *Elementary Principles of Acting*. Samuel French. New York.

MUSIC

Community singing is one of the most interesting activities of the boys and girls. There are a large number of collections of songs available, both Jewish and non-Jewish, for this activity, together with suggestions as to how to make the most of community singing.

The National Recreation Association, New York, N. Y., has published a book on community and assembly singing, the price of which is sixty cents. This contains suggestions for methods of introducing and developing community singing with a comprehensive list of the best song collections, separate songs, stereopticon slides and books having to do with the planning and conducting of simple festivals and holiday celebrations.

The National Play Bureau of the Federal Theatre Project, New York, N. Y. has published a list of sixty-six plays with synopsis and comments and a list of forty-four selected adult operettas for which amateur performance rights may be obtained by purchasing the number of books required for the cast, the cost of which is ten cents each.

The following are good folk-songs collections:

Edgar, Marjorie, *Old Songs and Balladry*. Girl Scouts, Inc., New York. 1930.

Twice 55 Community Songs Green Book. With accompaniment. C. C. Birchard, Boston, 1930. Vocal edition, twenty-five cents.

The Jewish Welfare Board, New York, N. Y., has issued a number of collections of modern Palestinian songs in English and Hebrew, Yiddish folk songs, Jewish operettas, song tableaux; price of each collection, ten cents.

The Bureau of Jewish Education, Chicago, has issued little books of Jewish songs by Harry Coopersmith, price five or ten cents. The pamphlets contain festival songs, songs for the Sunday schools, and Sabbath chants.

The Hebrew Publishing Company, 79 Delancey Street, New York, N. Y., has published the early Yiddish operettas, words and music which contain some of the best popular Jewish folk songs; especially recommended are the operettas of Goldfaden.

A. W. Binder, Bloch Publishing Company, New York, N. Y., has composed and published a number of song books and a number of operettas dealing with festival themes. He has also issued a number of Palestinian song books.

The following are good Jewish song books:

Coopersmith, Harry. *The Jewish Community Songster*. Bureau of Jewish Education. Chicago. Twenty cents.

Altman, Sholem. *The Judaean Songster.* Young Judaea. New York. 1934. Seventy-five cents.

Bible and Festival Song Book. With music. Bureau of Jewish Education. Chicago. One dollar.

Goldfarb, Israel. *The Jewish Songster.* United Synagogue of America. 1928.

ARTS AND CRAFTS

The Industrial Arts Cooperative Service, 519 W. 121st St., New York, N. Y., is a valuable source organization. Their Catalog No. 3, 1936, gives prices for all material necessary for the different types of arts and crafts. This service has suggestions for different types of arts and crafts such as woodwork, basketry, metal work, stagecraft, marionettes, puppetry, etc. It also operates a loan library where certain designs on the various classifications can be borrowed.

The following are suggested books:

Chicago Board of Education. *Manual of Artcraft Designs.*

Best, Adolfo. *A Method for Creative Design.* Maynard. 1935.

King and Pessels. *You and Your Camera.* Girl Scouts, Inc. 1936.

Perkins, Ruth. *Handbook on the Use of Crafts.* The Womans Press. New York. 1934.

Good bibliography on arts and crafts together with list of sources for arts and crafts supplies. Sources classified as follows: colors, charcoal pencils, crayons, yarns and looms, leather and leather-working tools, blockprinting tools and materials, basketry and rush weaving, metal crafts, clay, underglazes, and kilns.

The Board of Jewish Education, Chicago, has published a number of mimeographed pamphlets, written by Tudros Geller, on artcraft projects for the various Jewish festivals.

The Associated Talmud Torahs, 330 South Ninth Street, Philadelphia, have also published material on arts and crafts.

The following are suggested books on Jewish arts and crafts:

The Jewish Welfare Board. *Applied Arts and Handcrafts*. New York. N. Y. Thirty-five cents.

Comins, Harry L. and Reuben Leaf. *Arts and Crafts for the Jewish Club*. Department of Synagogue and School Extension of the Union of American Hebrew Congregations, Cincinnati, Ohio. 1934.

Best book on Jewish arts and crafts at present. Detailed manual of instructions on carving in bas relief, constructing decorative objects of wood, decorative metal work, applique work, upholstery work, leather work, clay modeling, pottery, lino cuts and wood cuts.

SOCIAL SERVICE

The publications of the Boy Scouts, the Girl Scouts, etc. contain a very large number of suggestions as to projects that adolescents may engage in that are of value to the community.

An interesting description of some of the more important ways in which youth has served to meet some of the human and civic needs is *Youth Serves the Community*, by P. R. Hanna. D. Appleton-Century Company. 1936.

The Union of American Hebrew Congregations. *Some Hints for a Philanthropy Committee. Projects About the Jewish Community*. Cincinnati, Ohio. Fifteen cents.

Some of the larger federations of philanthropy and social service publish material that is useful in educating the adolescents in the needs of the Jewish community. Among these organizations are the following:

American Ort Federation, 212 Fifth Avenue, New York, N. Y.

Zionist Organization of America, 111 Fifth Avenue, New York, N. Y.

The Jewish National Fund, Inc., 111 Fifth Avenue, New York, N. Y.

The Joint Distribution Committee, 100 E. 42nd St., New York, N. Y.

The Federation for the Support of Jewish Philanthropies, 71 W. 47th Street, New York, N. Y.

The American Jewish Committee.

The National Conference on Jewish Relations.

The American Jewish Congress.

The Anti-Defamation League.

Through the Zionist Organization and the Joint Distribution Committee it may be possible to secure the names and addressess of Jewish schools and high schools in Palestine and other parts of the world with which the Junior Synagogues may correspond.

Some suggestions as to methods by which the adolescents may cooperate in communal activities are contained in the following:

U. S. Office of Education, Committee on Youth Problems. *Youth: How Communities Can Help.* Bulletin, 19936. No. 18—1. Washington: Government Printing Office.

Edmonson, J. B. "Plans for an Improved Social Life." National Education Association, Department of Superintendence. *Social Change and Education.* Thirteenth Yearbook. 1935: 64—78.

Gosling, Thomas W. "Youth Trains for Service." *Nation's Schools.* 18: 18—21, October, 1936.

PERIODICALS

It may be well for the library to include the following periodicals:

Occupations, published monthly by the National Occupational Conference.

Play, a monthly bulletin for recreation leaders, published by the Epworth League, 40 Rush Street, Chicago, Ill. $1.00 a year.

Program Service, Boys' Club of America, 381 Fourth Avenue, New York, N. Y.

Recreation, published monthly by the National Recreation Association, New York, N. Y.

The Social Frontier, 525 W. 120th St., New York City.

Youth Service, American Social Hygiene Association, 50 W. 50th Street, New York, N. Y.

Youth Leaders' Digest, Youth Service Inc., Peekskill, N. Y.

The Jewish Frontier, The League for Labor Palestine. 275 Seventh Ave., New York City.

The M. L. A. Review, published quarterly by the Metropolitan Leaders Association, New York, N. Y.

The New Palestine, weekly publication of the Zionist Organization of America, New York, N. Y.

Opinion, edited by Dr. Stephen S. Wise, a monthly devoted to Jewish letters.

The Reconstructionist, the Society of Advancement of Judaism, 15 West 86th Street, New York City.

Young Israel, published monthly by the Union of American Hebrew Congregations.

The Young Judaean, issued ten times a year, monthly from September to June, inclusive. Young Judaea, Inc. New York.

The Youth Leader, published by the Department of Synagogue and School Extension, Cincinnati, Ohio.

Jewish Social Studies, National Conference on Jewish Relations, 55 Fifth Ave., N. Y. C. A quarterly devoted to sociological and statistical studies of contemporary Jewish life and relations.

Contemporary Jewish Record, The American Jewish Committee, 461 Fourth Ave., New York City. A review of events and digest of opinion.

Religion. A digest. Protestant, Catholic and Jewish thought. 55 East 10 St., St. Paul, Minn.